MARTIN M. BROADWE
Training Consultant

WILLIAM F. SIMPSON, CPCU
Management Training Manager
Kemper Group

THE NEW INSURANCE SUPERVISOR

ADDISON-WESLEY PUBLISHING COMPANY
Reading, Massachusetts · Menlo Park, California
London · Amsterdam · Don Mills, Ontario · Sydney

Library of Congress Cataloging in Publication Data

Broadwell, Martin M
    The new insurance supervisor.

    Includes index.
    1. Supervision of employees. 2. Insurance
companies–Management. I. Simpson, William F.,
1927– joint author. II. Title.
HF5549.B8545 368'.0068'3 80–22170
ISBN 0-201-00896-3

Third Printing, July 1984

ISBN 0-201-00896-3
    CDEFGHIJ-AL-8987654

PREFACE

Over a decade I have used the first and second editions of the book, "The New Supervisor" as part of the education and training of hundreds of insurance supervisors and managers from both the company and the agency-broker side of the business.

The challenges, gratifications, and problems these supervisors experience are at once universal and unique, timeless and as current as today. Whether the supervisor is part of a large company made up of thousands of employees or an owner of a small agency of four or five people, objectives must be planned and employees must be recruited, selected, trained, and motivated to perform well in the demanding testing ground of the marketplace.

These universal, timeless challenges exist against a specific insurance backdrop of vigorous competition, computerization, and other techno-logical innovation and an environment in which "publics" as diverse as employees, shareholders, customers, producers, claimants, and regulatory authorities register increasing expectations of the industry.

These challenges and expectations need the expertise of trained, professional supervision and management if they are to be met and realized. We need able technical, professional, and clerical personnel, to be certain, but we also need the means to identify, to train, and to develop competent supervisors and managers from among our under-writers, raters, statisticians, coders, claim adjusters, engineers, and typists.

It was this need that motivated me to collaborate with Martin M. Broadwell, the author of "The New Supervisor," to adapt its solid description of such supervisory skills as planning, communicating, appraising, and interviewing to the unique mechanisms, technology, and environment of our business.

Cary, Illinois   W.F.S.
February 1980

CONTENTS

PROLOGUE

All the books in the world won't prepare a person adequately for that first day—or even the first few weeks—as a supervisor. The first time we have responsibility not only for the job but also for the people doing the job, it can be an awesome thing. But the job becomes rewarding when it is done properly, and it can be done that way if we avoid certain mistakes.

The purpose of this book is to help keep the new insurance supervisor from doing wrong some things that others did wrong when they became new supervisors. There is very little theory in this book, but that isn't to say that practical application of many theories isn't here. People do not act theoretically; neither can they be supervised theoretically. The new insurance supervisor has gone too far to be satisfied with just theories, no matter how good they are or how practical they have proven to be. What he or she wants to know is "What do I do right now with *this* problem?"

We hope that this book will help answer that question.

1

A NEW ATTITUDE TOWARD THE JOB

A NEW ROLE

Supervising others can be fully understood only by those who do it. This doesn't mean it is mysterious or deep, it just means it's hard to explain—like describing chocolate cake to someone who has never eaten cake. That first day on the job can be frustrating, and many supervisors have been heard to say, "I didn't know how well off I was. At least I knew what I was doing." And therein lies the problem. When we become supervisors, we must realize that we've taken on a new role for which we are qualified; but our training may range from complete to sketchy depending on the company or organization we work for.

There was one thing about the old job—whether we were a rater, underwriter, computer programmer or whatever, we knew what to do and when to do it. In fact, we may have been picked as a supervisor in the first place because we could rate, code, sell insurance or settle automobile claims better than anyone else in the work unit. Someone, probably a department or branch manager, looked at us and decided we were pretty good at our job and seemed to have the qualities needed by a good supervisor; and so they promoted us to supervisor. Now we have the job, but what do we do? Where do we go from here?

We are understandably concerned about our ability to do the job. As a supervisor, we now have people working for us whose typing, coding, or underwriting we really can't do for them. Our primary job now is to see that they do the work. No matter how slow they seem to be, or how poor their attitude may be, or how much they foul up the job, our role is still not to do the work ourselves but to get them to do it.

Remember when we used to gripe about the boss doing things wrong? Remember those sessions around the coffee machine when we and the rest of the employees used to really let the boss have it (behind his or her back, of course)? Well, we're the boss now, and they're talking about us around the coffee machine. This means we are going to have

1

to start looking at things differently. *Our job now is to worry about the job*. This doesn't mean our people aren't important—we've already seen that they are the ones who do the claim adjusting, rating, or engineering inspections—but it means that we must learn to think about both the people and the job and not let either one become more important than the other. And as we will see time and again in this book that's a never-ending balancing act.

Let's look at a simple example: Susan comes in red-eyed and obviously has a problem. As the story unfolds, it sounds something like this:

> Susan's having family problems. She and her husband haven't been married very long and this morning they had an argument. The husband was pretty hateful and said some pretty mean things. Susan has decided to go home to Mother, and wants to take the afternoon off so she can go home and pack before her husband gets there. The only thing is, she can't afford to lose the pay (now that she's on her own) and wants to work through the next several lunch periods to make it up. This means actually showing her time as worked this afternoon, but not showing her as having worked through the lunch periods. She says she is willing to work the equivalent of five or six hours for the three or so hours off so she won't lose the money. The truth is, we can't afford to let her go (even without pay) because of the heavy work load today; but as distraught as she is, there's no telling how she will react if we tell her she can't go. Also, if we say no, she'll think it's just because we weren't willing to let her make it up during lunch periods. She's waiting now for an answer and needs it immediately so she can call her mother.

Well, what do we do? The problem is real and important to Susan. As supervisors we are expected to make the right decisions. Suppose we let her go, with or without pay; what will we tell Jim when he comes in next week and asks to leave early to go deer hunting with his friends? How will we explain to Jim the difference in our treatment of the two situations? Suppose we don't let him go; how much production can we expect to get out of him for the rest of the day? How will we explain the loss in production to our boss? What will our decision do to the morale in the office?

NEW WORDS—NEW MEANINGS TO OLD ONES

As we go along we will see approaches to solving this kind of problem that are better than just doing what our instincts tell us. But for now, let's say that we must learn a new vocabulary. At least, we must learn new meanings for old words. They are going to be key words and key meanings throughout our entire careers as supervisors and managers. They are going to be the things that we spend our time thinking about, worrying about, and making decisions about. Words like *management* take on a different look now. *Money, time, objectives,* and *cost/benefit* aren't strange or bad words anymore. We can't make decisions just on the basis of emotions, or even on the feelings of the people involved. We must make the decisions on the basis of good job management and in light of what's good for the organization. That includes the feelings of the people but not only the feelings of the people.

All of this says that the word "production" should take on a new, vital meaning for us. We aren't responsible for just things anymore; people and money and time and production have suddenly become inseparable. And remember, we ourselves are no longer supposed to do the thing we were the best at—getting the job done. And remember, too, we are still learning to do this new job of supervising people. Of course, there are some basic rules: treat employees as we would like to be treated; remember that they are human beings. The basic human

courtesies are more important than ever. Now we may not even be sure how we would like to be treated in a similar situation. Knowing what we do about production needs, work scheduling, profits, and the bosses' demands means that we might want to be treated differently from those who don't know about these things. And suppose we treat Susan and Jim considerately and kindly? That's a good thought, but what do we do with their problems now, and what do we do about getting the job done?

Though this may sound a bit callous, it really isn't. It just means that being a supervisor changes things for us. It changes our outlook and presents us with new problems. It changes our perspective and gives us a bigger picture to look at. It doesn't take the human element out or make it any less important. It gives us more factors to consider when we make decisions. It does, in fact, give us the right and opportunity to make decisions that were not ours to make before. As we said earlier, the job becomes important now, and all these other things are part of getting the job done. It doesn't make us any less interested in people; it makes us even more interested in people, but in a different way. We are interested in them because they are the ones that make us look good or bad. In a sense they have been entrusted into our hands, and we have an obligation to see that things go well for them. But the job has also been entrusted to us, and we have an obligation to the organization to see that the work is done so that *all concerned* will profit.

A DIFFERENT GROUP NOW

The supervisory role has been referred to as the lonely role. It looked simple enough when we were working for the boss and he or she was making all the decisions. It didn't seem too bad when he or she seemed just to be there. As a matter of fact, we remember when we used to say, "Boy, that's really having it made. We do the work and the boss gets the credit and the money and the office!" This job looked pretty easy when we were the Susans and Jims, but somehow it doesn't look now the way it did then. Even Susan and Sally and Jim and Chuck look different to us now. But they haven't changed, and we haven't changed. So what's different? The job is different. The responsibility has changed. Our viewpoint has changed. And let's face it, our loyalties have probably changed, too. Whether we like it or not, the people working for us don't see us the same way now that we are the boss; and we really can't afford to see them the same way, either. A few supervisors have been able to make a go of it by telling the old group that nothing has changed. They have continued to go on break and eat lunch with them and gripe with them and criticize the organization with them. They knock the department manager with them and handle discipline problems and fire some and promote some and avoid getting into trouble with the group—and through it all they still get the work done. But for every supervisor who takes this route and succeeds there are a hundred failures to show that it is a dangerous route to take. Being a regular guy or gal is nice and all right, too—but only if the phrase means that you're still a regular guy even though you are the boss. You can't give up being the boss just to stay a regular guy.

The important thing is that we belong to a different group now. We have to give up some of the pleasures of being part of the old group and accept our position as the boss. As the boss, we belong to the group that is made up of the other supervisors and managers. We don't have to associate with them, but we have to communicate with them on their level (which is our level, too). We still have to communicate with those who work for us on their level (which is not our level now). As we look out over the group that works for us, we must say, "We are a group that must stick together, perform as one unit and meet the organization's objectives. But even though we work as one, I must be the leader. I must set the pattern of leadership by letting them be a part of setting objectives and developing performance standards; I must lead by giving them as much authority as possible so they can do their job with a minimum of interference from me; I must see that they are trained thoroughly and that ultimately they develop their full potential; I must see that their needs are met; but I must do these things as the boss, not as just one of them."

How do we accomplish this without being snobbish or conceited or overbearing? It isn't easy, but it is far from impossible. In the next chapter we will see some examples of how it can be done successfully.

CONCLUSION

The role of a new supervisor is quite a change from whatever else we have been doing. Coming from within the company or organization will cause one kind of problem; coming from outside will cause another. In either case, though, things are going to be different from now on. The purpose of the job is different. Viewpoints are different. Like it or not, we're part of a different group now; we're part of the managing effort, rather than a part of the technical or clerical effort. Our job is now to get the typing, rating, coding, or claim adjusting done through others, not do it ourselves. Instead of griping about the supervisor, we've become the supervisor. Instead of griping about policy, we must implement the policy. Instead of waiting for someone to appraise us, we must appraise the performance of others. This goes on and on, because we've taken on this new role. It takes some getting used to, but we can do it. Many have preceded us in mastering this supervisory role successfully. We can master it too.

EXERCISES

1. Individual activity: Let each person write down how he or she got to be a supervisor. (What do they think the processes were—in the minds of the decision makers—that led to the promotion?) Even if the person was hired from the outside as a supervisor, what led the organization to choose this person over another—as a supervisor?

2. Subgroup activity: Divide the group into two subgroups. Have one subgroup list what might be typical viewpoints of technical or clerical employees toward the job of supervision, and the other subgroup list how a newly appointed supervisor might feel about supervision the first week after taking the job. Record the lists in separate places.

3. From the above lists, let each person vote "Agree" or "Disagree" on each item in each list. Do the majority of the group members agree with the employees or with the supervisors?

4. Group discussion: In a group discussion, come up with a list of criteria or factors that ought to be taken into consideration in selecting a person for the job of supervisor. Let the whole group get agreement on as many things as possible. (The dissenters should be answered by those who are in favor of the item under discussion.)

5. Small-group activity: Working in several small groups, give the subgroups two or three of the items from number 4 and have each decide how their items could be measured. (Be sure that each item is measured well enough—by their suggestions—so that each person's work can be distinguished from that of the others.)

6. Subgroup activity: Divide the group into subgroups. Have one group represent typical technical or clerical employees and the other group represent typical first-line supervisors. Have them look at the following words and give their "feelings" about each of them.

After each individual does this, each subgroup should try to come up with a consensus on each word. In discussing them afterward, see if there is even a difference in the definition in the words themselves. The words to be discussed are:

Time off	Cost/benefit	Work
Management	Performance standards	The boss
Profit	Performance appraisal	Production
Objectives	Money	Overtime

2
A NEW ATTITUDE
TOWARD THE SUBORDINATE

As new supervisors, one of the most difficult things for us to accept is the fact that some of our employees might be able to do our job just as well as we can. In fact, in different circumstances, one of them might well have become the supervisor. What made the difference? Brain power? Probably not. In sheer ability to think, most of us come out very close to the middle range, even though we like to think of it otherwise. The fact that we are now supervisors doesn't reduce the brain power of those we supervise, or mean that we necessarily have more than they have. What about knowledge of the job? This varies, of course, because many new supervisors know their former job better than anyone else (which may well be a major reason they were selected for the supervisory job in the first place). On the other hand, as new supervisors, we may know less about the job we're supervising than someone else. For example, if we were promoted from adjusting worker compensation claims exclusively to supervise a different work unit that might also include adjusting some liability-type claims, this could be the case. Overlooking the matter of luck or influence, the only thing we can say for sure is that the new supervisor gets the job because some higher-level manager thinks he or she can handle the job of getting work done by directing the activities of others.

RECOGNIZE THEIR ABILITIES

So what, then, should be our attitude toward those who work for us? The important thing to remember is that it is to our advantage, as well as company's to use our employees' talents as much as possible, leaving less and less of their job for us to do! It's rather poor management of time, people, and talent to let brain power go unused, or to let experience and knowledge of the job be wasted. And the chances are pretty good that whether or not our people use these things is the result of actions that we take or don't take. In a sense we can think of our people as being a huge storehouse of brain power and technical knowledge of the job. The only catch is that we must find the right keys to give us access to this tremendous asset. Not every key will work every time, nor will every key work on every individual; so we spend much of our time looking for the right keys and trying them out when we find them—all of which adds to the satisfaction and challenge of being a supervisor!

SUBORDINATES HAVE NEEDS

Those who work for us have more than brain power, job knowledge, and experience; they have certain needs and anxieties that occasionally work against them but can be made to work for us. For example, if their needs are being met on the job, then we have found a good source of motivation. On the other hand, if there are very strong needs that are not being met on the job we aren't, no matter how hard we work, likely to have much success at motivating them. It isn't enough to just say, "Well, I have problems, too, and I don't let it influence my performance." That may or may not be true, but in any case, we still have to recognize the problems that employees bring to work with them. This doesn't mean we have to excuse poor performance caused by outside problems, but it does mean we have to accept the fact that an employee has those problems and that they may affect his or her work.

But outside problems aren't the only things that cause employees to have anxieties; there are many things right on the job that will bother them and can cause them to develop additional problems. For example, just the fact that you're new to the job as supervisor will cause certain anxieties. The employees may not be sure how they will relate to you now that you are the supervisor. They don't know how they will fit into your thinking; they will worry about your opinion of them and the impression you will get of their work. They will have to start all over again competing with the others in the organization to establish a position in your esteem. These aren't necessarily large problems, but they are real and you must consider them.

Not only will employees worry about how you will see them but they will also be watching you to see how you act under certain conditions. What will it be like when there is an important rush job to be done? Will you be the kind that puts the screws on tight, or will you just relax and not worry about deadlines? What happens when an employee does something wrong? Will you just say, "Forget it"? Or will you get angry and embarrass him or her in front of everyone? What happens when other departments or groups interfere with your activities or don't meet their deadlines to you? Will you assert yourself or will you let them run roughshod over you? Your employees want to know these things about you and will be anxious about it until the questions are resolved or until you have acted in such a way as to assure them that they don't have to worry about these things.

AMBIVALENCE—LOVE AND HATE

One of the strange things about being a supervisor is that we have to learn that it's possible for our people to love us and hate us at the same time. Perhaps these terms are too strong, but they identify the problems brought about by the phenomenon of "ambivalence." This simply means that because we represent two different things to employees, it's possible for them to feel two different ways about us. As a supervisor, we represent authority—something that tells them what to do and what not to do, hence a threat to their satisfaction. As a supervisor, we represent the employees' means of getting ahead, getting a raise, solving their problems, being recognized, or being told how to do things more easily—hence real security. Just as we are simultaneously a comfort and a threat to them, so they can like us for what we do for them and dislike us for what we stand for. This shows itself in the employees' reactions to the ways in which we give them assignments. For example, if we just tell an employee to write a letter to a claimant without specifying the objectives of the letter, he or she may justifiably complain, "I don't know what you want me to do." If, on the other hand, we give our underwriters what they consider to be too detailed instructions on their limits of authority, they're apt to accuse us of oversupervising them and not giving them adequate opportunity to develop underwriting judgment. Again, our job as a supervisor is to recognize that this phenomenon exists, and to look for ways of using it to our advantage.

BOSSES ARE NICE PEOPLE

Often we find ourselves in the peculiar position of seeming to defend our "bosshood." Very early in the game we must realize that there is nothing wrong with being a supervisor, and we should never feel the need to apologize for it or defend it. Every organization, at almost any level, must have someone who is in charge. For whatever reason, we are that person in this situation, and it's up to us to accept that fact and begin to act the part. As a matter of fact, if we find ourselves continually being too defensive of our role as the supervisor it probably indicates that we aren't being a very good one. ("Look fellows, I hate to sound like the boss, but we've got to get this underwriting report out today.")

Interestingly enough, while we may try to hide or avoid the fact, our employees pragmatically see us as the supervisor. Whether or not we act like it is our choice, but they still know we are in spite of whatever we do. All this means is that we should get the work done by being the supervisor, not by trying to be a friend or a buddy, or trying to bribe the employees into doing what they are being paid to do. The problems of supervision arise not because we are the boss, but because we don't live up to the full role of the supervisor—or, in a small minority of situations, because we exploit our authority as a supervisor. While we have every right to be the boss, we have no right to use this fact as the only means of getting the work done. We can't demand that the employees respect us, and although by demanding it we can get work out of them for awhile, such action breeds a negative reaction that sooner or later comes back to haunt us. One of the quickest haunting jobs happens when we have acted haughtily for some time only to find ourselves suddenly in a crisis situation where it's ultimately up to our employees to pull our chestnuts out of the fire. Often they "innocently" let these chestnuts burn! So how should we act? Later in this book we will deal with some specific behavior that has proven to be very satisfactory in setting up the right relationship between the supervisor and the employee. Right now we are just suggesting that somewhere between the two extremes of trying to hide the fact that we are supervisors and exploiting our position lies the happy ground of being successful at it.

WE DEPEND ON OUR PEOPLE

Whether we like it or not, we still must depend on our people to accomplish the goals of the company or organization. We can do only a certain amount ourselves, and generally the more of the work we do, the poorer job of supervision we do. Sooner or later we must get the work done through the people the organization has given us to do it with. That is why our attitude toward these people is so important. We may not think we have enough people, the right people, or enough time for enough training, but it is still up to us as supervisors to get the work done with these people at this time under these conditions.

And this brings us to this critical thought: These are also the people that will make us look good or bad in bottom-line terms. Let's face it, these are the people who can ultimately make us or break us as supervisors. Our ability to use their skills, our ability to motivate them to perform, and our ability to get them to think and do the way the company wants are the things we will be rated on by the branch manager or agency owner when appraisal time rolls around. So their performance will have a direct and important bearing on our rating as a supervisor.

THEY GET OUR JOB

Finally, our attitude toward our people is important because we have an obligation to our management to see that those who work for us develop the right attitude. *It is from their ranks that our job and others like ours must ultimately be filled, and the way we train them, challenge them, and treat them will determine whether or not the organization has enough properly trained supervisors to replace us when we move on to better things.* Our attitude toward them will probably influence the attitude they have toward their subordinates when they are promoted. Equally important, it may determine their attitude toward the organization as a whole, both now and when they become supervisors. It is just as shortsighted to think of our people only in the jobs they fill as it is to think of ourselves only in the job we fill. It is certainly an indictment of us if we have failed to develop anyone under us who is capable of handling much, if not all, of our work when we are out of the office or when we are moved to another assignment.

CONCLUSION

What have we said about our attitude toward our employees? We have said we must realize that they have a storehouse of brain power and technical experience for which the successful supervisor will find keys. It is ultimately through the abilities of the subordinates that the job must get done. We've seen that the subordinates have certain needs and anxieties which they either brought to the job or developed after they got there. In fact, we may well contribute to the problem, because to them we represent both a threat and a source of security. In the process of getting the job done, we've got to be careful not to try to defend or apologize for being the supervisor. We don't need to defend it or hide it, but neither do we want to exploit it, because the people who work for us are the means by which the organization will meet its objectives. These are the same people who will determine to a large degree just how well we do when we are appraised, because our bottom-line responsibility as a supervisor is really one of getting the job done through them. Finally, these are the people who should be able to move into our job when we are moved on to other jobs. Our attitude toward our technical and clerical staff will largely determine our actions toward them; hence it will determine how well they are able to take over when we leave.

EXERCISES

1. Group discussion: Have the group brainstorm ways in which technical or clerical employees have problems that are exactly the same as supervisors. This isn't limited just to the job activities, but includes their home life, community, future planning, money, etc. Record this and then discuss why sometimes supervisors tend to think their people shouldn't have personal problems—or at least should not let them interfere with the job.

2. Using the list above, have the group decide whether these problems we all have in common actually do interfere with supervisors performing their job as boss.

3. Group discussion: Have the group brainstorm ways in which technical or clerical staff have problems that are not like those of typical supervisors. Record this and decide whether these problems interfere with work. Can supervisors let their "nonsimilar" problems interfere with their work?

4. Individual assignment: Let each person make a list of the ways "ambivalence" is displayed in the work place. Find places where the supervisor is criticized by the employees for doing something, but where there would also be criticism if the boss failed to act. We discussed this in this chapter, using the example of close supervision versus not enough direction.

5. Small-group activity: Divide the group into two subgroups. Have one subgroup think of ways in which supervisors can and should use their positions as supervisor to their advantage. The other subgroup should think of ways and times when letting it be known

that we are the boss can be harmful. One group is discussing the advantages of using the position of supervisor and the other is listing the disadvantages, both with specific examples.

6. Group discussion: Discuss ways in which the job couldn't get done if our technical and clerical employees decided to do just what they were told to do and no more. Give some specific examples.

3

A NEW ATTITUDE
TOWARD THE BOSS

BOSSES HAVE THEIR OWN PROBLEMS

One of the sharp realities that confronts us soon after we become supervisors is the fact that our problems are often compounded by our employees coming in with their problems, leaving us less time for our own. This really ought to be a loud and clear message for us: *If it's true for us, it must surely be true for our boss.* In fact, it is very true. Even though we sometimes don't like to admit it, our manager is usually working on problems of greater magnitude than ours. Indeed, the manager could be concerned with a whole cycle of work—rating, coding, underwriting, policy typing, and billing and collection. In a sense, our problems at the first level of supervision are really also our manager's as are all the problems of the other people who work for him or her either directly or indirectly. Even if our boss doesn't have problems that are more important, at least he or she has more. It behooves us, then, not to add our problems to our manager's burdens, or at least to avoid adding any more than we can help.

The objective we must attain is to make very sure that we understand the boss's role and our own role and where the dividing line is between them. We need to remember that just as it's our job to get a certain portion of the work done through other people, so it is our boss's job to get things done through us front-line supervisors. If we get the mistaken idea that the boss is just sitting around giving us work so he or she won't have anything to do, let's stop and realize that our people could feel the same way about us! And they would probably also be wrong! Another point to remember is that our manager has the responsibility not only for our decisions but also for the decisions of other subordinates, and any bad decisions he or she makes have more important results than ours do. This certainly doesn't mean that our boss is going to check everything we do anyway, so we can forget about using good judgment as doing the job right. It means just the opposite; it

means that the better judgment we use and the more completely and thoroughly we do our supervisory job, the better job our manager can do. Using our best judgment helps our boss handle the bigger, broader problems because we have brought him or her a little more time when they don't have to worry as much about our mistakes and poor judgment. And the better our manager does the job, the better the final results are for us. Even if we don't get the credit for a particular job well done, we are still in the unit, department, or agency that got the good results, and in the long run it will pay off for everyone concerned.

MANAGERS HAVE FEELINGS TOO

Much of the supervisory training we will get as new supervisors will understandably tell us that our people have feelings, anxieties, problems, needs, etc.—a fact we all readily agree with. But sometimes the unfortunate implication is that we as supervisors and managers don't have any feelings or problems, or at least that we aren't supposed to let them show. Actually no one argues that bosses don't have problems, and most will agree that we need to be careful about letting these problems affect our behavior. Even so, we have to admit that our concern with our problems does show sometimes. We can't help it, perhaps. But if we admit that we have feelings that show sometimes, shouldn't we also admit that our manager must also have problems and feelings that may show in his or her behavior from time to time? As a matter of fact, our boss has just about every problem and anxiety that we might have: worries about home, family, money, chances for promotion, relationship with the others on the same level, and being a good leader and administrator. And of course, like ourselves, our boss is concerned about the relationship with his or her own manager. Often the boss has put money into the company or organization and could be out of a job and broke besides. We're kidding ourselves if we think we have a monopoly on problems, either business or personal.

We tend to forget that our manager also has a boss, or maybe even several bosses. He or she may be responsible to one or more owners of the company, agency or organization. As much as we'd like to think that our manager always worries about us first, we'd be more honest to admit that we don't do that even for our employees. When the going gets rough around the department or branch office, we can't help thinking "How's this going to affect me?" Often we don't start to worry about those under us until after we've answered that question. More than likely this is so with most managers, including our own. But that's all right as long as we recognize that the boss is only acting human and is reacting about the same way we would under similar circumstances. That's no excuse for our manager to treat his or her people wrongly in such situations, but at least we recognize the reason for the behavior and so may know how to act in return.

THE MANAGER IS ONE STEP REMOVED

One problem that confronts our manager is that of being one step removed from the job and activity of our employees, just as we're one step removed from our manager's boss. This means there's a chance our manager is not getting a full view of the situation, just as we may not be seeing things from the same angle as the one up the line. The chances are pretty good that our manager won't see things the same way we see them, especially things about our people and their work. Remember that he or she must see all of this through the information we provide and from personal observation, then relate it to the bigger departmental or branch picture he or she is looking at. Also, our manager has certain charges and objectives from his or her boss, and other supervisors and units to worry about besides us and our employees—all of which understandably can cause our manager to see things quite differently from the way we do. So realistically there shouldn't be any great mystery if our boss's interpretation of these things differs from ours.

Take the matter of appraising our technical and clerical staff. Being one step removed, our manager may fail to see the potential we see in some of our people. He or she may be judging them on past performance and fail to realize how rapidly and well they are developing. Since we see them every day, we have a much better chance to see how they are developing new skills and how much better they handle responsibility than they did a month or even a few weeks ago. Our boss's opinion of the person we have in mind may be based on an untypical incident of past performance that created an unfavorable impression, so our boss understandably might not believe that there has been a change. By the same token, our boss may find it hard to believe that one of our former "star" raters isn't performing as well as he or she should be. We may have an employee who was rated as excellent or superior at one time but for some reason is just not performing up to the standard that his or her abilities have led us to expect.

Our manager may be dubious about our most recent evaluation of the technical or clerical staffer because the previous rather glowing record doesn't seem to bear us out. To make matters worse, since he or she must base a judgment on less information than we have, our boss may form opinions on incorrect information or even for emotional reasons, or may base an opinion on something overheard on the elevator or at the coffee machine or something heard about the employee through someone else. While such information is not reliable, it may be all that our manager has, especially if we have failed to keep him or her properly informed. We all form opinions based on the information we receive, and our manager is no exception.

WE ARE ONE STEP REMOVED, TOO

Our manager isn't the only one who is apt to form opinions on limited amounts of information. We, too, are oftentimes guilty. We must be careful not to pass quick judgment on company or organizational policies before getting the whole story. Policies that are set one or more steps above our manager will likely lose some of their meaning and reason for existence by the time they get to us. For example, a decision made several levels up to convert from manual handling of a job to computerized handling may in fact be the only alternative open to the company. Understandably, each layer of management sees decisions in relation to their department or unit; we see them in relation to our job and the jobs of our employees. Each of us has a unique sized window to look out of, so each sees something different from what another sees.

Policies that are not fully explained or understood may appear to be unreasonable. When we fail to get the whole picture before we talk to our employees, we may say that the company or organization is making bad decisions. If we don't know all the facts involved, we just don't see things as we should. Does this mean that the department or branch manager must tell us everything he or she knows and the reasoning behind every decision that is made? Of course not, although we often act as though we expect it. At some point we need to develop enough confidence in our management to realize that they are usually making decisions on the basis of more and better information than we have. If we still have some doubts, then we should try to find out more about the reasons behind what is happening. This is the place to request, not demand, the information. Our manager is obligated to help us as much as possible but cannot spend all his or her time trying to justify everything the organization does. We should realize that we wouldn't want our employees using up our time in this manner. We don't mind explaining; in fact we should make an effort to tell as much as we can about the rationale behind organizational policies and procedures. But this doesn't mean that the only way to motivate our employees is to spend most of our day defending and justifying the organization's policies.

One problem we can have as a new supervisor is that we may be starting from scratch in finding out just what the organization's goals really are. This is particularly true if we were hired as a supervisor from the outside. Because we are new, we naturally lack quite a bit of background on why the company or agency does certain things in certain ways. This can work a hardship on us because we may find ourselves going off in the wrong direction without even realizing it, then having to reverse ourselves and perhaps lose face with our employees in doing so. Few companies have organized orientation programs that will bring us up to date on all the things we need to know about the background of the branch, the department, or the organization as a whole; so each day we must hit the ground running in order to catch up. We can't just sit back and say, "Well, now that I'm a supervisor, it's up to the organization to train me in all the things I need to know." When we accepted the job as supervisor, we also implicitly accepted the responsibility for a large amount of our own development, including finding out about how and why things are run the way they are. The task is a difficult one, but it must be accomplished if we are to make a success of the new job.

CONCLUSION

As new supervisors, we must develop the proper attitude toward our manager and his or her job. We must recognize that our boss has to worry not only about us and our job, but also about the other managers and supervisors working in that branch or department. At the same time, our manager is human and will have many of the same business problems and anxieties that we have, and they may show occasionally on the job. He or she also works for someone else, and so is likely to worry some about his or her own position in the company or organization. And since our manager is one step removed from our technical and clerical employees and their work, he or she gets much less information about them than we do, and so may reach different or even wrong conclusions about which of our employees are good and which need improvement on the job. At the same time, we are one step removed from our manager's manager, so we may get the wrong impressions about the policies and decisions that are made at their level. We can't expect our manager to explain every detail and every reason for every act, so we must develop confidence in those who make the policies and ask about only those things we need to know more about in order to explain to our employees. Finally, we will find it challenging to learn all that we need to know about the background of the organization and its people when we first make supervisor. While the company or organization should provide as much training as possible, the responsibility is still primarily ours to do as much self-development as possible. Because there is so much new information and knowledge to be learned and not much time to learn it, a good relationship with our manager will go a long way toward building mutual confidence to sustain us across the gaps in our knowledge.

EXERCISES

1. Small-group activity: Break the group into several small groups and have them discuss and list ways in which we cause our managers problems without even realizing it sometimes. Don't think of it just in terms of one person working for another; rather think in terms of a first-line supervisor working for the next higher level of management, be it a branch office, a department, or an agency. This information should then be shared with the entire group with a discussion of how these things could be avoided.

2. Small-group activity: In the same small groups, make a list of the ways the next higher level of management makes problems for the first line of supervision without realizing it. Again, discuss ways in which this could be overcome.

3. Group discussion: Develop a list of problems the next higher level of management has in being the boss that the first line of supervision does not have. Remember, this second higher level of supervision has problems that are people problems, too. In many ways there are similarities, but in some ways there are differences. List not only the people problems, but also think in terms of organization problems. These should be recorded and kept for further discussion.

4. Small-group activity: Have small groups discuss at least two of those problems discovered in exercise 3 above, with the idea of finding ways the first level of supervision could make life easier for the next higher level of management. What could we first-level supervisors do to ease some of the problems listed here?

5. Group discussion: Communicating up and down the line in any organization is a never-ending management problem. The first level of supervision is at the bottom of the management hierarchy. This means that they will often be the last level of management to get information about objectives, policies, procedures, and problems. The group should generate a list of topics that are likely not to get to the first line of supervision until after implementation has begun at higher organizational levels. The idea is to look for things that happen or are decided upon that actually may begin to go into effect before the lowest level of supervision finds out about it in the normal operation of the business. For example, a departmental or branch budget is set, some higher-level management promotions might be made, or there might be a reorganization of the top level of the company, branch or agency. List these things for later discussion.

6. Small-group activity: Divide the group into two subgroups. Have one subgroup debate the other on at least two of the items or topics identified above, one side taking the position that there is no reason for higher management sharing this information with the first-line supervisors before going ahead, and the other taking the position that it is essential that first-line supervision be aware of the proposed changes or other decisions before they begin to be implemented practically.

4

SUPERVISORS' RELATIONS WITH THEIR COORDINATES

GROWING UP IS ESSENTIAL

It sometimes surprises and demoralizes new supervisors that there is so much bickering and infighting going on among the other supervisors who are their coordinates or peers. If we're thoughtful about this, we'll react by saying to ourselves, "Why don't they grow up?" That's the real problem. The ability to get along in a work situation where everyone has the same general working conditions, the same manager and the same organizational policies to work with is a measure of our maturity. It all seems pretty ridiculous, because most of us would rather work in a situation where everyone gets along with everyone else and does their job and where nobody complains about anything. But that's a dream world that just doesn't exist. Do we just give in, then, and cynically prepare for battle?

Not if we want to get our job done and help the organization toward its objectives. What's important is that all of our ultimate objectives are the same (or should be). We want the department or the branch office to prosper, the profit and expense objectives to be met, more money and other resources to be made available, and what we have used efficiently so that there will be raises and promotions. The challenge is that while we all may have the same long-range objectives, the short-range ones seem to differ—even to be opposed to one another. Each supervisor is assigned a task, given technical and/or clerical employees to do that task, allocated money to carry out the task, etc. Because each task seems different in its purpose and subobjectives, conflict soon arises. We each become intent on reaching our objective with our money and our staff. Each of us has his or her own problems to solve and own means of solving them. The conflict arises when we get so intent on our own problems that we lose sight of the organization's overall objectives and problems. We resent anyone who seems to get in our way while we are striving to get where the company or

25

organization wants us to go. We forget that the organization wants us to get there together with the other supervisors, not with their bodies strewn out behind us!

GET THE JOB DONE, BUT . . .

Sooner or later some supervisor will emerge as the leader of a "Let's get-along" movement. Why shouldn't we be the one? We can do our part in seeing that things run smoothly and still get the job done. We really don't have many choices in our relationships with our coordinates or peers. We can try to get the job done by working against them, caring little for how they react or feel; or we can try to get it done by issuing edicts like, "Forget about them, let's get the job done." Or finally, we can get the job done through a cooperative effort, taking everything into consideration. When we think about how counterproductive it is for everyone to spend time bickering, it's easy to see that the last alternative is the only practical one.

To get the job done by working against the supervisors we should be working with can produce some ghosts that can haunt us pretty badly later on. We may think we've done our job well, but most people resent being walked over and can react vindictively; and when they hit back, it's usually with a harder blow than we gave them.

The forget-about-them technique can often be tempting. "If they don't want to cooperate, just let them go their way, I'll go mine." It seems so simple, but it rarely works. All it takes is for the boss to say, "Did you check this out with George in underwriting?" Or "Will this fit into the time slot with Helen's project on renewal billings?" Now we've got problems. We've either got to admit that we failed to check it out, try to alibi (*a lie by I*), or go back and take the chance of having to do much of our job over, this time working with those whom we've deliberately ignored.

All of this matter of cooperating sounds fine, but making it work is a continual challenge. There are some built-in contradictions. For instance, we want our people to be loyal; we want them to respect us as their leader; we would like to hear them say that they work for the best department in the agency or the company. That's great—or is it? Loyalty is fine, but it can also work against us. People often find it easier to be loyal to a small group than to a large company or organization, so they develop strong feelings about the immediate work group, even refusing promotions to other groups or being disgruntled when they are moved somewhere for the betterment of the overall organization. This means their loyalty really isn't to the organization, but to a supervisor or a group of fellow workers. This isn't bad; but it can become bad when it causes the overall objectives of the company or organization to suffer. When our technical or clerical staff begins a type of over-zealous competition with other units to the extent that it brings about hard feelings or causes one group to take advantage of another, then the ultimate results can be bad.

Another problem is that resentment, which is often the beginning of jealousy, can build among supervisors. We don't like to admit that we are jealous, but, for example, let the manager spend too much time with another supervisor and we begin to wonder if the boss likes that manager or his or her work better than ours. Again we see the immaturity coming out. Lack of confidence will produce the same results. We may feel that we can't really compete on the performance level, so we start to look for other things to make up the difference in our relationship with our manager. We may resort to a whisper campaign against a fellow supervisor; we may begin ruinous infighting; we may even find ways of telling the manager that all of the other three supervisors in the branch have some weaknesses. We may tell the boss about foul-ups, real or alleged, that he or she might have missed if we hadn't brought them up. Of course, the manager shouldn't think better of us for doing such a thing, but even if he or she does, we have probably weakened our position in the organization. One of these days we are going to find ourselves needing some help from someone we have criticized to the boss, or hoping that the boss doesn't find out about a mess we are desperately trying to get straightened out. At that time, we may look longingly for friendship and understanding from the other supervisors and not find it!

MAKE IT WORK

How do we get the job done? How do we get the cooperation that it takes to get along and get the work out at the same time? Perhaps the one word that comes the closest to being the key is "communication." The old saying, "We're usually down on what we're not up on," is just as true here as anywhere else. We need to know what's going on in the other work units or groups, and it's worth our time to find out. We'll appreciate our fellow-employees' jobs a lot more if we know something about their problems and the reasons for what they're doing. And the same is true about their appreciating what we're trying to do in our unit, they need to know where we're trying to go, how we plan to get there, and whom we have working to get us there.

We need to anticipate possible conflicts and problems before they have gone too far to be stopped. We need to get into the habit of giving out as much information as possible to those we work with, including other supervisors. We should learn to communicate. When we find ourselves saying to someone, "But I told you . . ." we're actually admitting that we don't know very much about communicating. Telling rarely is communicating. One good practice is to get into the habit of writing memos and notes to the other supervisors we work with, letting them know what projects we are working on that might need their help or that might either conflict with or complement theirs in some way. The key point is that they will be in a better position to help us if they know what we're doing. Equally important, if they know something of our operation, they will be better able to answer questions that arise from their subordinates about how their work relates to ours.

Another practical habit to get into is checking with our coordinates when there is something we don't understand about their job or operation. If one of their employees gets into a misunderstanding with one of ours, don't just go and jump on somebody but go calmly and get some facts. We aren't obligated to start a quarrel whenever one of our people has a problem with someone from another work unit. That's building the wrong kind of loyalty through misguided example. Our employees may think we're being forceful for doing it, but we aren't really helping them, ourselves, or the situation by storming around the department or the agency telling other supervisors off. And remember, we shouldn't even idly say that we're "going to get this straightened out once and for all," implying that we will jump on somebody about this. That, too can build a wrong kind of narrowly combative loyalty. In the long run, our staff will respect us more if we provide a smooth working environment for them and a fairly harmonious relationship with the others with whom they must associate.

AVOID LEARNING THE WRONG THING

One more challenge we have as new supervisors is what we do around those people who have been in the organization for a long time and for one reason or another have grown hypercritical or even bitter. There can be a sort of "habitually negative" syndrome that affects some employees. They don't like certain policies that affect them; they don't like the way promotions are handled; they don't like the way their raises have been coming or the amount; they feel they should be higher in the organization or should be consulted more or should be making more money. Perhaps even worse, they may see us in our capacity as a supervisor as a threat to their own security. They may feel that the newer employees have a better chance than they do, so they will resent us and make life a little hard for us. Most of us can handle that, because it's fairly easy to see through it to the negative motivation. It's the same problem we faced in school when we made better grades than a classmate who had been considered the better student for a long time. It's like the time when, as a kid, we raced a person who was faster or older than we were and, for some reason, on this occasion just outran them. Paradoxically, the people who can give us the most trouble are those who do know their jobs and who are respected for their knowledge. One of them may even be the person who's been assigned to teach us some of the procedures. When this person has a negative streak or is bitter, it affects us a lot more.

What can we do about such a situation? The best approach may be to ignore it. Certainly we shouldn't try to correct the person or try any mindchanging. To start off with, we're probably going to lose the argument just on the basis of experience and knowledge alone. These people will know more arguments and more ways to offset ours than we'll ever be able to handle at our stage of supervisory know-how. So we'd be well advised to leave that approach alone. We could try to present another side of the picture as we see it, but even this has risks. In showing us where we've misinterpreted the data, they might "convert" us to their way of thinking. In the beginning at least, the best thing for us to do is simply listen and not respond to the negative attitudes of others.

Later, as we build more confidence or deepen our knowledge of the operation, we might try to deal more assertively with people who are like this; but at first probably the most practical advice is to let them alone. There is always the possibility that they're right, but in the beginning we really can't tell, so saying nothing will serve us better than anything else we do. Sooner or later we've got to come to our own conclusions about the organization, about the manager, about our particular work group, and about the specific job we're working on. The sooner we do it, the better, but we ought to make sure that it's our own thoughts we're analyzing, not those of the older and so-called wiser heads around us. Just as they have more information, they may also have more biases. At least we ought to wait until we've developed our own ideas and philosophy before we become defensive or start to disapprove of the way the company or agency is run.

Another thing we're going to have to do eventually is develop our own standard of behavior. We may not realize it, but at first we really don't have a supervisory standard of behavior. We act like the employees around us; we ask them how we should feel about things, how we should act, and even what kind of action is preferable. At some point we need to ask ourselves, "Is this really me in my role as supervisor, or am I still just parroting what I've heard from other employees?" We need to decide for ourselves how we feel about the manager, the organization, etc., and it ought to be based on as much fact and experience as possible. Above all, it ought to be us.

CONCLUSION

Our ability to get along with the people we work with, particularly the other supervisors, is one test of our maturity. After all, we're all working for the same organization with the same long-range objectives. The advantages of working in a harmonious environment are obvious. In developing loyalties within our employees we need to be careful to see that they are built around the company or organization as a whole, not just to us as a person or to our small work unit. When we work with other supervisors under the same manager, we need to realize that in the long run cooperation is the key to getting the job done satisfactorily. Hostile aggressiveness or ignoring others in our work and planning may seem like a quick way, but it is not a sure way. The best way is to learn to communicate not by telling or dictating, but by being sure that fellow-supervisors get a memo or a note from us informing them what we're doing and suggesting ways in which cooperating might help both of us. Of course, these aren't the only times we need to communicate with them. We need to talk with them about possible conflicts or problems that might arise among our subordinates. But our getting together with other supervisors should be goal-oriented, not a "stage-managed" effort to build our prestige among our own employees. Our technical and clerical staff might enjoy our melodramatic confrontations with other supervisors, but in the long run that probably won't help the company or the agency. The thing that is most likely to help the organization is for us to develop a good working relationship with our coordinates so that the situation will be conducive to productive work by the units concerned.

EXERCISES

1. Group discussion: In almost any organization, there is some competition among the various units working for the same department manager. There must be some universal reasons why this happens. Develop a list of why it happens in an organization and why it seems to be common in any type of work unit. Record this list for discussion in the next two exercises.

2. Group discussion: Using the group's findings from above, decide whether the effect of this competitiveness is good or bad. In other words, if it did not exist, would the company or organization be better off or worse off?

3. Individual assignment: Let each person evaluate the list, and list ways he or she could avoid having each one of the bad results happen in his or her work unit. This can be a long assignment, and each person should consider each item. When all have, the group, as a whole, should discuss each item to find the simplest way to avoid destruction competition, in those cases where the members feel such competition should be eliminated.

4. Small-group activity: In small groups, develop a sample policy statement that might be put into effect in the company or organization that would deal with the problem of poor communication. This statement ought to be explicit enough to both describe what the supervisor should do, and what he or she should communicate to the employees. (This is a type of team-building exercise, and important to us. Each person should think in terms of what he or she would like to know, when they should know it, and how often there should be a review process for looking at the communications. The statement should also deal with the accountability for the communications effort, that is, who should be responsible for seeing that the communications effort is made, and what the consequences are for failure to do it.)

5
THE IMPORTANCE
OF GOOD COMMUNICATIONS

COMMUNICATING—GOOD OR BAD?

It's easy to tell supervisors they should be good communicators; it's much harder to tell them *how* to be good communicators. One problem is that we aren't always sure just what we mean by "good communications." The preacher who presents a great sermon gets rousing support (orally) from the congregation; but when someone asks what the sermon was about, very few may be able to answer correctly. The politician who holds an audience spellbound may find that he or she failed to communicate when the members of the audience go out and vote for someone else. As supervisors, we are most often transmitting messages that should produce some action (an underwriting analysis), change something (a coding procedure), or speak to the action that has already been carried out, if only to say that it was right or wrong. What is good communicating in this context of front-line supervision?

We might define good communication as getting the right message to the right source in an efficient manner. Notice that we said "in an efficient manner," not necessarily the cheapest, or the quickest, or the easiest. "Efficient" also means "correct." The reason for saying it this way is that so often we take the easy way out and just tell somebody something. But since our people are human and may forget, this isn't a very efficient method. Pretty soon we will find that the employee we told will have to be told again, that he or she is adjusting compensation claims incorrectly or has somehow gotten the purchase requisition procedure all fouled up. Perhaps another word we could use is "effective." "Effective" carries yet another implication; it implies that the message got through and the correct results have come from the action taken. When we send a message, we should think to ourselves, "It isn't enough to be sure that it can be understood; I must be sure that it will be very difficult to misunderstand."

FOUR ELEMENTS IN COMMUNICATING

We can understand communicating better if we break it down and systematically look at the parts or elements that go to make up any communication effort. In essence, there are four basic elements that we can look at—the sender, the receiver, the message, and the environment or conditions under which the message is sent. Each of these things affects the results, and the effectiveness of our communication depends on how well we as a front-line supervisor take each one into consideration. For example, the most powerful speaker you know will have trouble when the conference or meeting room is too cold or too hot, or when the employees are preoccupied with how they are going to drive home through a heavy snowfall. This doesn't mean that that speaker can't do a better job than someone else; it means that he or she could be even more effective under better circumstances. On the other hand, when the employee we're talking to really wants the information we're presenting and is eager to hang on to every word, our presentation can be pretty poor and still get across. But it could get across even better if we were doing a better job. When I'm bragging to the car pool about my success at fishing, I doubt seriously that I'm getting through very much, especially if traffic happens to be bad; but when I'm talking to an underwriter whose agent I've just seen at an agent's meeting, I can expect the message to get across much better. Finally, when my son wants me to pick him up from someplace so he won't have to walk home, he goes into much detail and even, uncharacteristically, repeats what he's said so there will be no misunderstanding.

Note that there is a difference in emphasis on identifying the breakdown point in effective communication. A different element can be involved in each case. In the fishing story, neither the subject matter nor the environment was conducive to successful transmission. In the example of talking to the underwriter about the agent, the message was very important to the underwriter for business reasons, and the receiver (underwriter) was ready to hang on to every word. When my son talks to me about giving him a ride, I may not be very interested in the message, but to him it is all-important. And it is important to him as the sender to see that I (as the receiver) get the message. There are several things to notice here about effective communication. First, widely different conditions can exist when we transmit information. Next, the sender and the receiver may understandably have different degrees of interest in the subject matter. The simple truth is that it is probably rare for the sender and the receiver to have the same feeling toward the message. But if we fail to take this into consideration when we try to communicate to someone, we may lose the message.

One problem we have is that as senders we always want to put the responsibility for successful communication on the receiver rather than accept it ourselves. We always react the same way when someone fails to get what we were saying. We think (or say), "But I told the claim adjusters. . . ." The first thing we tend to do is to rationalize that if the employee had listened, he or she would have gotten the message. And that is indeed rationalization. We are failing to accept the responsibility for taking all the communication elements into consideration. Did we realize that the employee wasn't getting the message or may not have been interested and that we should have done something to stir up that interest? Did we consider that the environment of a crowded, noisy lunch room might not have been the best place for good communicating? Were the doors to the conference room open and others listening in? Was the phone on our desk ringing? Was the receiver waiting to see the boss? Were there other distractions either in the office or in his or her mind? Was the receiver really just tolerating our conversation, waiting for the chance to begin his or her own monologue? Did we choose the right time and the right place to discuss the subject? Did we first pre-pare the receiver for the discussion by making it clear what it was we were going to discuss?

These are all important considerations, each one of which can help or hurt the effectiveness of our communications. We can't choose either to pay attention to them or ignore them; if we ignore them, they will still tend to disrupt our communicating efforts. What usually happens is that we use about the same approach each time, except in very critical situations. We say things the same way to different people, regardless of the circumstances or whether the person we're talking to is interested. We wouldn't dare approach the boss for a raise and promotion in the same manner we would ask for a sandwich in a restaurant, but what about the many times between those extremes when we probably should take a little more care in the way we choose our words and our approach? Unfortunately, the natural approach is to put things in our own frame of reference—on the basis of our interest, our vocabulary, our need for telling. What we should do, of course, is to put all of our conversation and other types of communication in the receiver's frame of reference, but this is a lot easier said than done. For example, even with a brand new underwriting trainee we unconsciously slip into jargon like "dec" (for declarations page of the policy which lists such information as name and address of the insured, etc.). *We are not likely to think in the receiver's frame of reference unless we make a conscious effort to do so.*

THE RECEIVER HAS A DIFFERENT FREQUENCY

We think in terms of our goals, our interests, our needs, and our problems—not the receiver's goals, interests, needs, and problems. When we communicate, we do it successfully by either tuning in on the receiver's frequency or getting the receiver to tune in on ours. Human nature being what it is, the chances are pretty good that both the sender and the receiver desire that the other make the change. But the sender generally has the message that needs to be transmitted, and so should accept the responsibility of seeing that both are on the same frequency. This is particularly applicable to us because, as a supervisor, we are generally expected to initiate job-related communication.

Perhaps one of the best things we can do before we try communicating is ask ourselves what frequency the receiver is on. In other words, "What is there about this message on increased underwriting authority that would make Fred think he wants to get it? It's important to me, but why should it be important to him? After all, Fred is a commercial underwriter and I know he needs it, but does *he* know it?" When we've decided what the receiver's frequency is, then we must put ourselves in Fred's place and decide whether we would get the message from the communication we're preparing. To put it another way, we must ask, "Is this the best way to get the message on coding changes across to Ruth? Will she really read my memo or this bulletin from the department manager? Will she read it carefully enough to see that it was meant for her or maybe that it might contain a new departure, somewhat different from what she has learned about coding in the few weeks she's been a trainee on the job?" There are plenty of cases on record in which important new policy changes have been carefully put into bulletin or memo form only to have the meaning and intent altered considerably by the time they have gotten down to the technical or clerical staff who were supposed to use them on a day-to-day basis.

BARRIERS TO EFFECTIVE COMMUNICATING

This brings us to the important point of looking at some of the barriers to good communicating. Take the case of losing the intent of a new policy or procedure by putting it into written form and sending it down through the organization. To an outsider, reading the letter for the first time, it may appear that this is clear enough and that there is probably no reason for a later misunderstanding. A closer examination, however, may show that many written communications go up and down through the organization every day, carrying too many insignificant details. Those who receive them have learned through experience that rarely does anything important relating to policy or procedure come to them in written form, and when it does, there will also be a special announcement made by someone else at the same time. In effect, the potential receivers say to themselves, "If it's really important, somebody will tell me without my spending a lot of time reading useless material." (This ought to also be a lesson for us first-line supervisors; be alert enough to catch important messages without having to be told by some other source.) We'll label the first barrier, then, as inadvertently hiding important messages among those that the receiver has learned aren't very significant.

The second barrier, which is related to the first, is sending unimportant messages at all. It doesn't make good business sense to send messages about which we may think, "Oh well, nobody ever reads these things anyway." It doesn't take us long to get into some careless habits writing with this background thought in mind. Equally pointless is the idea of writing just to move the responsibility to someone else's shoulders: "I did my part; I wrote a memo covering it." This, in fact, becomes an unnecessary message and is ultimately even a much more damaging communication than none at all. This becomes a third barrier if we consider that our motives weren't very honest in the first place. We aren't likely to work very hard at making a message clear if we have ulterior motives in sending it. After all, what we're really trying to do in such a case is hide or mask the truth, so what better way to do it than in garbled communication.

Even when we have the best of intentions we run into another barrier—overkill. It's so important and so vital that everyone get the message that we go into too much detail or give too many unrelated facts. As a result, the real message gets smothered by a lot of background information that belongs right there—in the background of the message, not in the foreground. The problem can come when we start to sell the idea instead of just giving out the necessary information. When we start selling, we almost always go too far, often raising questions in the receivers' minds about things that aren't really important to the subject we are discussing. They might be having second thoughts about our motives. Contrary to what may seem logical at first glance, it might be better to give a little disciplined, relevant information than a lot of unorganized and irrelevant information. Too much information can not only raise questions, but may also get the receivers to thinking about something that they are particularly opposed to or have already made some kind of judgment about. When they get to thinking about their emotional reactions, the real message can suffer, and maybe even get lost. Trying to get it across the second time will probably be much harder than the first because emotional barriers may have been raised.

This suggests yet another barrier to good communication—the unintended results we can get by not organizing the message skillfully. If we hide an important message on expense account procedures among unnecessary information, it can't help but get lost. By the same token, if we organize it so poorly that our field engineers or claim specialists get so confused trying to find out what we're really trying to say about personal use of a company car, we might as well not have sent the message in the first place. Let's do a little thinking about how to organize. It stands to reason that the more time we spend leading up to an important point, the easier it will be for the receiver to get lost or lose interest. So one of the ways we can organize the communication effectively is to get the important part of the message out as quickly as possible. Start off by saying what it is we are trying to get across. "We'll apply these rate changes starting October 1," or, "Starting next Wednesday, we'll use the new billing workflow." If nothing else happens, at least we will get the person's attention! Communication authorities tell us that the first and last things we hear or read are the things we remember the longest. This means that the closing should also contain either a summary or a conclusion or a call for some action. In another chapter we'll deal specifically with writing; for now let's notice one of the ways this barrier can work against most letter writers. When we write a letter, we say what we want to say, offer answers to problems, give out the necessary information, but then often don't know how to close. Instead of just stopping, we look for some artificial way to end it. Almost without exception, we use some kind of trite phrase that is impersonal and sound stuffy. "If we can be of any further assistance to you in this or any other matter, please do not hesitate to call on us." If it's true that we remember the first and last thing we read, then what will the reader remember about us? Not that we are willing to help, but that we are distant, and maybe pompous, and that we use form letters to send our messages! If there's nothing at all friendly and helpful by the time we get to the end of the letter, the reader isn't likely to believe it just because we use some worn-out phrase.

One more barrier we want to talk about is the matter of trying to communicate with people who have different slants or different kinds of information. This difference in viewpoint will cause the message to be lost or confused before it does its job for us. For example, when we talk to the nonsupervisory people who work for us about something the company wants, we have to remember that their views of the company and even their loyalties are quite different from ours. So we have to realize that they will likely receive the message as meaning something else if we put it in terms of "the company." Of course, education, experience, and other background factors play a big part in our ability to communicate and contribute to this same general barrier. The employee who is struggling to make ends meet and is worried about the next house payment isn't likely to get the desired intent of the message that says that the company's new long-range savings plan is a good investment even if it means doing without for the time being.

APPLICATION

Now let's go back and look at some of these barriers and see how they work in real life. Let's take the matter of hiding the important messages among the less important ones and consider the supervisor who sometimes finds it necessary to get important messages to the large number of people working for him or her but is unable to call large group meetings because of the nature of the job. A particularly important policy change has come up and it is necessary to get it to the people as soon as possible. The choices might be: (a) call the people in smaller groups until all of them have been covered, (b) pass around a memorandum to all of them, (c) appoint some of them to come in and get the message and then take it to the rest of the people, or (d) post the message on the bulletin board. What is our best approach under the circumstances?

First, let's make sure that we understand that in supervision there is often no clear-cut right or wrong way to do something. There are advantages and disadvantages, and the decision may come down to which alternative has the fewest drawbacks. So how do we get the new policy matter across to our people? Let's see what is likely to happen if we choose (d), putting the message on the bulletin board. If the board is like many, there may be all kinds of insignificant things there from lost dogs to cars for sale. But even if it is reasonably clean, the bulletin board offers several drawbacks. It gives us no assurance that all of our people will see the notice unless we contact them individually and remind them to look at it. But while we were telling them this, we could also have given them the policy message in the first place.

How about (b), having a memorandum passed around to all of the employees? This has the advantage of seeing that everyone gets the message at the same time and in the same words. But if there are likely to be questions, this isn't very good, because the people they will ask are operators like themselves who got their information from the same memorandum in the first place. Maybe the alternative to choose is (c): call in a group of keypunch operators, for example, and brief them, then have them take the message back to the rest of their peers. There are some real advantages to this idea, even though it sounds as though it would take the same amount of time as calling in all the people in small groups, since that's what we will be expecting the group leaders to do. The advantage of (c) is that we could have a chance to sell the opinion leaders in the work group; they will then be doing the selling of the new policy to the rest of the employees. In the long run, this might be our best approach. But here again there is the danger of having the employees get the wrong or confused story, since it will be coming from several people instead of one. This could be minimized beforehand by having the memorandum referred to earlier sent out with a note that there will be follow-up group meetings in which our keypunch operators can ask questions. If we do a good

job of briefing the leaders, our work is reduced considerably. The final choice is (a), do all the briefing ourselves. If we think there will be any problems about the operators accepting the policy change from one of their own peers, then we shouldn't hesitate to call the small-group meetings and communicate the policy change personally.

Let's examine the risk of "overkilling" the message. We have decided that a certain idea suggested by one of our marketing analysts is a great one, and we want to pass it on up the line to higher management. In an effort to prove what a good idea this is we decide it would be a help to include some background information on both the employee who came up with the idea and the need for the idea itself. We want to do a fair job of presenting both the employee and the idea, so we make some extravagant claims for the proposal. Of course, the results are obvious; we oversell. By the time the potential decision-makers wade through all of the nonessentials, they have lost interest, and we have lost a chance to sell a good idea and highlight the abilities of an able employee.

HOW CAN WE IMPROVE COMMUNICATION?

So far we have talked about the barriers and other traps that might hinder us from getting our supervisory message across. Let's look at some things we can do to get the job of communicating done effectively. First and foremost, we must get the message straight ourselves! After all, it was probably a vague idea about changing the location of a photo-copy machine or some other equipment when it all started. It wasn't full-grown and wasn't in any shape to be transmitted to our boss, our peers, or our employees. But if we plunge ahead and start to explain it to these people without first getting the whole picture straight in our own thinking, we're probably in for trouble and, ulti-mately, in for disappointment. The next thing we can do is to try selling the idea to those whose support we need. The fact that we think it is a great idea or plan doesn't necessarily mean that the supervisor of the nearby collection unit will agree, especially since he or she will have no place to put the equipment. Just trying to force our ideas down someone else's throat isn't likely to get us very far, but it will be a positive move to get the message out in the open. We sometimes try to sneak a recommendation or an unpleasant course of action by some-one hiding it between several pleasant or seemingly harmless things. The end result may be that we were successful—but our success was in hiding the idea. There's nothing better than tact when it comes to introducing changes or handling unpleasant messages. We should use it and whatever other human-relations tools we can, but in the end we must make sure the real message stands out and gets recognized. If we want to correct tardiness, careless work, poor writing, or bad attitudes toward customers, we'd better be sure that our employees know these are the things we are talking about. The situation may even be un-pleasant, but the message won't get lost!

Next, we should make certain the message gets there. It's not enough that we know what we plan to say or that we say it. It becomes successful communication only when the message gets to the receivers. How will we know that? Not just because we can say, "Don't you remember? I told you that we transmit computer input up to 12 noon." We will know for sure only when our operators repeat back to us what's been said. We want to know how they will hear the message, what it meant to them, and how they have interpreted our remarks. Successful supervisors and other communicators have different ways of getting this feedback. For example, some will simply ask the employee they're talking to what that person has heard. This tends to put the respon-sibility on the hearer, but is effective. Other supervisors may ask the employee to give them some feedback because they aren't sure they're communicating the message as well as they ought to. This keeps some of the blame for the misunderstanding (if there is any) on the super-visor. Still others try to get their feedback in the form of results from the message sent. They'll ask the hearers what action is planned as a result of the message they've heard. As the supervisor hears proposed action plans, such as having computer input delivered to the terminal operator no later than 11:30 A.M., he or she will not know just what the hearers heard and how it was understood. Whatever way we get our feedback, we must be sure that we don't rely just on our own confidence in ourselves as communicators. We may be good communicators most of the time, but we can probably improve our skill because we aren't as good at one time as we are at another. Also we may not be as effective with certain people and with certain messages as we are with others. As an example, we might include too much technical jargon in our messages to new employees.

The third part of good communicating is the ability to listen. Surveys show that supervisors and managers can spend half their workday listening. Listening is a skill that must be learned. Of all the skills of communicating, listening is the hardest to learn and the hardest to practice with any kind of consistency. As a matter of fact, the more we communicate, the more we can acquire bad habits. We get so used to hearing our own voice and so used to saying things in ways that sound good to us, that we forget everyone isn't always tuned into our voice or our message. Listening is more than just being quiet or passive. It means that we listen for content. We listen for meanings. We listen to see if our message has gotten through. We try not to get into the habit of hearing what we want to hear instead of what is really being said. When we are doing a good job of listening, we don't interrupt people or jump right in at the end of their sentence with a quick response because we can't stand silence. We pause, if necessary, until we've processed the information we've just received. We repeat the statements or facts if we've got any doubt about whether we heard right. We even ask for clarification if there's any chance of our misunderstanding something. Of course, we don't do this all the time, but we don't hesitate to do it if there's room for doubt. We learn to use effectively such phrases as, "Do I hear you saying that our billing cycle can take five days?" and, "Let me see if I have this straight . . . our Milwaukee branch manager will be here next week." and, "As I understand them, the points you are making in the claim analysis report are . . ." Again, we don't use these expressions all the time, but we aren't afraid of admitting that we may not be getting all that's sent.

Finally, we can summarize these skills in this way. They've been classified as the skills of good communicators:

1. Knowing the message
2. Knowing that the message got there
3. Listening

Remember, these are skills. They have to be learned, and as we move up in the organization hierarchy, we tend to fall back on the first one—know the message. We see ourselves as well informed. We've communicated a lot in our lives, so we naturally consider ourselves pretty good at it. We become self-satisfied and complacent. We tend to listen less effectively, and that can reduce our chance for good feedback. In the absence of this helpful feedback we have only our own, often limited, knowledge of the subject to fall back on—and we may not be as well informed on the topic as we think we are. The key conclusion to draw from this is that we can always be better at communicating.

CONCLUSION

Much has been said about communicating. In fact, it's the "much saying" that has made communicating so hard to practice effectively. We tend to talk more than to listen. We tend to talk before we fully understand the other person's message. To make things worse, most supervisors and others who are poor communicators often don't know it and may even blame others for not understanding what is said. Because there are always at least two people involved in any communicating effort, there is always the temptation for one to blame the other with neither accepting that blame. The solution to good communicating is not simplistic and not something that can be achieved overnight. There are skills involved and these skills are difficult to master. The best approach is for the supervisor to habitually apply ways of checking on how well he or she communicates so that at least one party in the communicating effort will be aware of the problem. The steps that were described are: know the message; know that the message got there; and listen. Listening is the most difficult part to learn, but it is an integral part of the whole process. It is through listening that we get the feedback for knowing whether the message got there. If we aren't very good at getting the message there initially, the knowledge that it didn't make it at least gives us a chance to try again. Somewhere down the line, we should improve our ability at getting the message there!

EXERCISES

1. Group activity: Have one person write down the following information; when he or she came to work with the organization, when he or she made supervisor and the name of one person working for him or her. Then have the writer whisper that information to another person, who whispers it to a third, and so on until the message gets around the room. Have the last person to receive it write it down. The originator should then read the information that was started around the room, and the last reads the information he or she received.

2. Individual activity: The activity above is one that can be used at parties to show how messages get garbled, but in this case we have a more serious purpose in finding out how to communicate more effectively. To increase this skill, do the following: Individually, each person should write down what his or her feelings were before, during, and after the exercise above. Next, there should be small-group discussions of the results. The findings should later be presented for the whole group to discuss.

3. Group discussion: Have the whole group decide whether any of the feelings listed in Exercise 2 exist in our communications efforts within the company or organization. Look for such comments as: "I wasn't interested." "I didn't care." "I thought it wasn't very important." "I couldn't remember." Have the group discuss these things and decide whether they make our communications poor within our real-world work situation.

4. Subgroup activity (a workshop): In every organization there are communication problems most of which could be either eliminated

entirely or at least improved. Have each subgroup look at the real work unit in which each of its members works, and decide what are the most serious communications problems within that unit or department. Spell out the problem in enough detail that it can be dealt with. Avoid describing your proposed solution; instead focus on defining the problem. (Of course, sometimes the problem definition can point toward a solution. For example, "The branch manager doesn't tell me anything," suggests that the solution is to have the boss tell me more, but it doesn't really pinpoint the exact problem. Why doesn't the manager tell me more? And how much more; what kinds of things; when should I be told? All of these aspects need to be dealt with.) The solutions will follow in the next exercise. Note: When problems are finally defined to the satisfaction of the subgroup, they should be put in priority order. Which of these problems are the most critical? Which must be dealt with first? Which would have the greatest payoff? And so on. Taking all of these things into consideration, rank the findings in order of importance.

5. Group exercise: Combine the problems from the subgroups and see if there is any similarity among the top-ranked descriptions of communications problems. Look at those at (or near) the top of most lists and decide how best to tackle them. Before this discussion ends, a decision should be made to take some kind of action or to recommend to the company or organization what action to take. Consider only one problem at a time and don't try to solve them all at one meeting. Other problems can be considered later.

6

SETTING UP THE WORK (PLANNING AND ORGANIZING)

As we have already seen, our job as supervisors is to get work done through the people who work for us. We do our most effective supervisory work when we deal with the problems of getting the overall job or task accomplished, rather than doing the job ourselves. Though we have the direct responsibility for the clerical and technical employees and how they do, except in a few instances we still are not supposed to do their work ourselves. Of course, emergencies arise, but we're talking about the normal activities expected of a supervisor.

SUPERVISORS AS MANAGERS

Earlier we made a distinction between "supervisor" and "manager." In our context, a department or a branch office manager directly supervises other supervisors. For our purposes in this and the next chapter we are going to change our use of the work "managing" slightly to talk about the supervisor's job of managing. Since the usual general definition of a manager is "one who gets the job done through people," we won't do any harm if we use the terms interchangeably. Any supervisor has certain managing responsibilities, and we want to see what that means to us, the new supervisors.

Everyone other than the technical or clerical employee probably has some managing to do. The only difference between the first-line supervisor and the head of the company or organization is the scope and responsibility of their managing assignments. A chief executive of a large insurance company may direct thousands of employees, whereas the owner of a small insurance agency may be responsible for two or three employees. Basically, every manager, whether top executive or front-line supervisor, has four managing functions to perform:

Planning

Organizing

Directing

Controlling

We'll discuss the first two in this chapter and the last two in the next. While all supervisors perform all of these functions, the extent to which they do each of them will usually depend on their level in the organization. For instance, top executives would probably spend much of their time on planning for the next several years, while first-line supervisors understandably would devote most of their time to directing and controlling the activities of the typists, statisticians, or raters they supervise. Since all supervisors have all of these functions, let's see what they mean to the new supervisor.

PLANNING

First, let's be sure we understand something about all of these functions because each is something that is done as a part of the job of super- vision. While we should learn each as a skill and be aware of the fact that we are doing it, we shouldn't be overawed because it has a fancy name or label. The chances are pretty good we'll perform some of each function either by design or by accident. So when we talk about planning, we're talking about the everyday supervisory job—how it's done, what will be done tomorrow, where we hope to go from there.

Planning is by far the most important of all the activities we've listed because everything else results from it. In plain language, it is the means by which we decide in what direction we want our group to go. The process can be performed carefully or haphazardly. The in- teresting thing is that even our doing nothing will still produce a result! The organization will still exist, tomorrow will still come, and the em- ployees will do something, right or wrong. Most experts agree that planning is the most important of all the supervisory or managing functions, and this is one reason why the company or organization will not stop just because we fail to plan. It may well get off the track or head in the wrong direction, but it will still struggle along.

Another reason for the importance of planning is that it's much harder to correct the results of poor planning later than to do it correctly in the first place. The results of poor planing can be disastrous, and, unfortunately for the ego of the new supervisor, they usually show up more quickly for him or her than for the higher-level management. When top management makes a mistake in planning, it can take many months or even years for it to come to light. When the first-line supervisor makes poor plans, it sometimes is only a matter of hours before the results are known. If an executive decides to spend more money on advertising to boost the sale of a certain insurance policy or service, it may take a year to see whether the campaign was a success. If a supervisor plans his or her work force incorrectly and has too many people off during a peak demand period, the resulting slowdown in production will be known before the day is over.

HOW AND WHAT TO PLAN

How do we as supervisors plan our work? Obviously we want to consider whatever alternatives are available to us and select the best one, all things considered. Too often new supervisors mistakenly think of planning as deciding to do—or not to do—one certain thing. Good planning always takes into consideration the possible alternatives, weighs them carefully, then selects the one with the most cost/benefit potential. There is a caution here, though: Don't try to find the perfect solution or the one that has no drawbacks. There seldom is such a plan. In fact, we may have to settle for the plan with the fewest drawbacks because none of the plans is completely satisfactory.

We form our plans by making four basic decisions:

1. What is to be done?
2. Who is to do it?
3. How is it to be done?
4. When is it to be done?

Now let's take these one at a time and see how they fit into the day-to-day job of supervising.

1. *What is to be done?* We should have this definitely in mind before we go on to any of the other questions. For example, it isn't enough to decide that we are going to give the people some more training, then go out and find someone to do the training. We must first decide exactly what training is needed, how much of the training we can do ourselves, how much can be done by someone else, and how much can be left for later. If we aren't careful,

we'll find ourselves trying to carry out plans that weren't very definite to start with; this can result in a muddled effort to make something work that didn't have a good probability of success in the first place. Summarized, the rule here is to be sure that we know exactly where it is we're going before we start to go there. It isn't necessary to write all our plans down, but it helps us understand what we are going to do if we record on a note pad a positive statement of at least the major goals or objectives which we've agreed on with our manager. Of course, the plan may change as we go along, but at least we have something to change. Otherwise we'll end up making our plans as we go, changing those, probably repeating our errors, and in general frustrating ourselves and our employees.

2. *Who is to do it?* Part of planning is to determine whether this is a project for all your employees, for just a few of the senior staff, or perhaps for one individual. If it is a one-time job, there can be an advantage in having only one or a few experienced employees working on the project. It's easier to keep up with a nonrecurring objective or assignment if only a few people are involved. It will probably require less training time if veteran employees are used. On the other hand, if the work is the kind that will continue to be a part of the responsibility of our work unit, then our planning should include deciding how soon we want everyone to learn the new work.

There is an important training consideration here: If we aren't careful, we may let a job or task just gradually come into being. No one is ever really trained for it, but finally everyone is doing it—probably not very well. We may have it in mind that one of these days we'll do the training, but we keep putting it off until a more convenient time which never comes. A basic fact to remember about training is that like everything else on the job it must be planned for. Left alone, it will either not happen or be done poorly. The good supervisor plans for it to happen and be done well!

3. *How is it to be done?* Once a goal or objective has been decided and agreed on, we still have to decide how it's going to be met. This decision has to be considered at every level, but especially at the first level of supervision. Policies about the work will most likely be set at a higher level of management, perhaps by a senior executive, but decisions about the actual work are usually made at the first level of supervision, the point in the organization where

the work is to be carried on. However, the decisions may not always be made here because some supervisors give up some authority to their bosses. (These same supervisors often complain that they don't have enough authority to carry out their jobs, when in reality they didn't use authority assertively when they had it.)

Policy-setting is sometimes actually done unconsciously, because we can set policy by doing nothing. If we don't come up with firm policies on such matters as overtime, appraisals, performance standards, and promotions—and act on them—precedents will begin to set the policies for us. For example, if we intend to do a job without adding employees we may be inadvertently setting a policy for more overtime toward the end of each project or job!

4. *When is it to be done?* The final question to be decided has to do with one of the most important ingredients in successful planning—time. While the obvious conclusion is that the completion date is the most important consideration in time, this is only part of the story. No deadline is missed suddenly. Long-range—annual or longer—plans often fall through because of poor planning by the month, week, or even by the day. As first-level supervisors we might not be primarily responsible for the long-range objectives of the organization, but we often are much involved in the identification and execution of shorter-range plans. So meeting these short-range objectives is the most important "time" aspect of our role in planning.

Understanding the plan

It may seem obvious, but no plan is very good if it isn't understood by the employees affected by it. The reason for raising this point is our later tendency to blame someone else when a plan begins to go awry. The first thing we should consider is whether or not the planning included safeguards against misunderstanding the plan. Were the employees informed? How were they informed? Were they told once, or did they get an opportunity to ask questions, seek additional information, and generally get familiar with what was expected of them? When appropriate, did employees have written reference materials to consult later?

This sounds like something that would be done only when some major operation is undertaken. Not so. Our employees need to know what's expected of them even in a small, one-hour assignment.

Remember, our people are understandably concerned with the day-to-day aspects of their job, so they will expect all types of job assignments to be clear and understandable.

Who's watching the clock?

Something that should concern us as supervisors is the fact that since higher management is interested in the "big picture" (i.e., the long-range objectives), they understandably may not be watching the short-range objectives nearly as closely. This means they may do no more than skim over an occasional progress report, always keeping an eye toward the final completion date. If we first-line supervisors aren't careful, we may be the only ones in our company or organization watching the short-range dates. However, we can be sure a lot of managers will be looking when it's too late to do anything at all about it!

Sometimes at first-level we may get the wrong impression that all levels of management are watching everything and that we're small cogs in a giant wheel. But if we let ourselves be deluded by this thinking, we could be heading for trouble, especially with short-range objectives and plans. Even though our senior managers seem to be watching over our shoulder, they still expect us to watch the day-by-day progress of the work. For example, if an annual objective is to reduce absenteeism, higher management will be concerned with quarterly or perhaps monthly reports in order to spot trends, but we and other first-line supervisors must react to who does and doesn't show up every day.

Objectives and policy

Planning, then, is a function of management in which we in effect contribute to the future of the company or organization in those operations for which we are held responsible. In the process of planning we decide where we are going (the objective) and how we intend to get there (the procedure). Some have compared this to a ship taking a trip. The objective is the destination of the ship, whereas procedure is the minute-by-minute course the ship must take to get there. In a sense, planning is the rudder that steers the ship. The supervisor doing the planning controls the ship, and without planning the ship has no rudder.

While we won't deal with it in detail in this chapter, we should learn quickly that the more we take our technical and clerical staff into our planning effort, the more likely we are to reach our objectives. Since we are most often involved in short-term planning, we are setting short-term objectives, usually with short-term implementation of procedures. These may well be everyday type things that our employees know as much (or even more) about than we do. Getting them to assist in setting deadlines is a good way to get commitment to these deadlines, and getting them to participate in laying out the procedures or ground rules is also a good way to motivate them to work according to these procedures.

A brief word about controlling

In the next chapter we'll talk in detail about the function of controlling, but we need to mention it here because planning and controlling are closely associated with each other. The supervisor controls according to the planning that has been done beforehand. For example, budgeting is a type of planning, but the budget itself also serves as a control. While it is being prepared, the budget is part of the planning function, but once an operation has begun, it becomes a control device.

Other examples might be quality control or service standards. Determining the organization's policies or procedures on quality or service is a basic part of planning. When they go into operation, they serve as controls. The importance of all of this is that we should actively support the use of budgets, standards, and controls, because it is through them that the desired end result is reached. They not only direct our way and tell us when we've reached the objective, but they also give us standards and check points by which to measure our progress along the way.

ORGANIZING

So far we've talked about a part of what is necessary to set up the work, but there is a function called "organizing" that also plays a big part in getting us to the final objective we have set for our work unit. "Organizing" is a pretty broad term and generally includes two things: the structure of the organization we have set up to do the job or task, and the people in this organization. Since higher management usually decides on the structure of the overall organization, we'll emphasize the part of organizing concerned with matching the formal structure and people. First, though, let's establish that we aren't talking about something big and complicated when we use the work "organization." We're simply talking about any group of people who have joined together in the work context to get something done that they couldn't get done by themselves. This applies to the small work group like a policy typing unit in a branch office as well as to an entire organization of thousands of people operating in all the states or in various countries. The same general principles will apply.

In Chapter 9 we will talk in detail about interviewing prospective employees, so we won't go into that here. However, since a key part of organizing includes staffing the organization, we should realize that when it comes time to fill a vacancy in our group, we will be expected to do an employment interview. Also, since the prospective employee will be working in our organization, we should look forward to meeting and finding out as much as possible about him or her. Many new supervisors, however, dread this phase of the job. A little knowledge of how to conduct the interview—and a little guided experience—should cause these fears to disappear or to diminish considerably.

Right person—right job

The major objective of the staffing phase of organizing is trying to match the potential of the employee with the requirements of the job. Unfortunately, we often find that through inept staffing we end up making ourselves and our employees frustrated and ineffective. For example, we may do poorly at matching an employee's skills and interests with a job, then later blame the employee for poor performance. We should really blame ourselves for our own faulty judgment!

Getting the right people to do the right job makes sense from several standpoints. Obviously, employees who are doing jobs for which they are well suited have fewer frustrations, see that they are contributing to the organization, and feel that they have a chance to be recognized. As a result, they are likely to be motivated to do their best and will be reasonably well-satisfied employees. From the supervisor's standpoint a lot of our problems are solved beforehand, because the employees' strong motivation should reduce absenteeism and turnover and increase productivity. We should then have more time to handle other phases of our supervisory job. From the company's or organization's standpoint, it not only gets value for wages paid, but it also gets a good picture of us as supervisors in the process. When our people perform well, it naturally reflects favorably on us. Note, however, that a mismatch between employee and job can make all of these things come out unfavorably.

Another aspect of organizing, with which we will deal in detail in Chapter 10, is training. It isn't enough to try to get employees and their jobs matched as well as possible; we usually must make up some difference between the employees' "going in" knowledge and skills and the job requirements. This can best be done by training. Of course, given enough time and patience employees will learn on their own. Many do, but this is rarely the most efficient way or the most practical approach from the organization's standpoint. Not only do we need to have the employees know their job, but we also need to know that they know how to do their work. Training gives us this knowledge because we see that they have had an opportunity to learn the skill. If it's good training, we will see them actually demonstrating their proficiency. Then if they still do not do their job properly, we can look for some cause other than lack of training.

CONCLUSION

We have often defined the supervisor's job as getting the job done through other people. A portion of the supervisor's job includes some functions that are usually classified as "managerial" rather than "supervisory." They can have many different names or labels but we'll classify them into four key functions—planning, organizing, directing, controlling. Two of these, planning and organizing, have to do with setting the work up; the other two have to do with getting the work done. The world of work is full of sayings about having a goal or objective, but the one that says, "If you don't know where you're going, any road will get you there," best describes the continual challenge of planning. Many organizations drift because they don't really know where they want to go. Supervisors should think continually in terms of planning. As simple as this sounds, it isn't easy to do with all the other things that are going on around the office or department. Once we've decided what to do, it's equally important to see that the right people, be they technical or clerical employees, are doing it. This comes under the function of organizing. It's not enough to plan; we must act on that plan. In simple terms, it's a matter of the right employees doing the right thing at the right time. Any time the supervisor has responsibility for the organizing of this function, it's important that he or she pays thoughtful attention to it, rather than just let things be done as they always have been.

EXERCISES

1. Group discussion: Develop a list of results that the organization must plan for at least five years ahead. To how many of these do we directly contribute with inputs that might help in the decision-making? Should we and could we contribute more than we do? Record this list for later discussion.

2. Group discussion: Develop a list of results the organization cannot plan for more than a month in advance. To how many of these things do we contribute with specific inputs that help in the decision-making? Should we and could we contribute more than we do? Record this list for later discussion.

3. Small-group discussion: Have half of the group take the list on long-range planning and the other half the short-range planning list. In smaller subgroups within these halves, decide what information is needed for each of the results or things planned. Go into as much detail as possible, even to listing forms or reports that are considered, if applicable. When the subgroups are through, let each half compile its findings.

4. Group discussion: With the lists from Exercise 3, try to determine how much the long-range planning is dependent on the short-range results. Compare the two lists to do this. Also, see if there is a similarity or overlapping in the lists. (This exercise can do much to show the relationship between short- and long-range planning.)

5. Individual activity: Each person should examine his or her own organization or work unit and decide how it would be best organized if it was just now being created. The objective is to decide how many people would be required, what their qualifications would be, who would report to whom, etc. In other words, make up an organization from scratch to do what is now being done.

6. Group activity: Take one of the organizations worked on in Exercise 5 above and let the whole group decide how it would be organized if it were done for the first time. This means selecting one the whole group is familiar with, or maybe creating a new organization to do one of the tasks the organization now does. Note that one of the requirements is to find out what the goals, plans, and services for that operation are. (The end product or service ought to be the same as it is now—or better—so that the group can see that if we were starting over from scratch, we'd probably do things differently.)

7

GETTING THE WORK DONE (DIRECTING AND CONTROLLING)

All supervisors can view their job as that of getting the work done through other people no matter how many or how few the people they supervise. Planning and organizing (discussed in Chapter 6) set the stage for the next two functions, directing and controlling. The best of plans and the best organization structures won't do the work by themselves. Only our employees can accomplish the work, and we must direct them in doing the work and control the efforts they put forth while doing it. In some cases planning and organizing will be done at higher levels in the company, organization or agency, whereas directing and controlling are usually done at the first level of supervision. So, as new supervisors we must be especially sensitive to the functions of directing and controlling.

DIRECTING

Of all the functions we perform as supervisors, directing is by far the hardest to master. Directing involves people, and people are complex, differing from one another and even changing within themselves from one day to the next. Our employees' needs vary as do their ambitions; and as these things change, so does the way a person may react to a given situation. This means that just about the time we think we have predicted how a certain policy typist will react to a certain situation, his or her reaction may change because of something we may not even be aware of (at home, at church, at the Little League field, etc.).

But the situation isn't hopeless. We can improve our ability to predict how employees are going to react to their environment. There are some recurring ways in which people react. This means that there are some things we can do that will give us a more predictable result, even though we are working with employees who are quite different from one another in job experience, education, interests, etc. Once we

have found out about these ideas and techniques, we can incorporate them into our "management philosophy." Let's look at some of these knowledge and skill areas and see how we can apply them to our supervisory relationship with our employees.

Facets of directing

There are three broad facets of directing—leading, communicating, and motivating. Each is a skill which is built on some basic principles.

Leading Let's discuss leadership first. What is leadership? Ask a dozen employees and you'll probably get a dozen different answers. It is a vague quality but one that is recognizable in supervisors or managers who have it. (More accurately, we can usually recognize the results of its presence, if not the quality itself.) Perhaps the easiest way to define leadership is to say that it is "the ability of a supervisor to inspire employees to work hard to achieve the goals of the company or organization." This achievement of organizational goals by employees is measurable even though identifying leadership traits in a particular supervisor might be more difficult.

We know with certainty that the idea that leaders are born, not made, is out of date. All of us can be better supervisors than we are today, and there are things we can learn that will produce better results in our work units. There are skills of leadership that can be learned and practiced. In fact, there are some identifiable characteristics that are shared by people who have been rated as good supervisory leaders, and we can develop these characteristics as we get more experience and training.

For example, successful leaders usually have the ability to see other people's points of view. They don't necessarily agree with those viewpoints or give in to them, but they have some empathy for the positions taken. They are sensitive to other people's problems and know why people feel the way they do. Successful supervisors sense how what they say will be taken by other individuals. They probably know how their employees will react to certain things that are done; and when the reaction is different from what they expect, they may even be able to analyze why it's different. Perhaps above all, successful leaders don't automatically attribute every undesirable behavior to "bad attitude."

Another characteristic of good supervisors is the ability to see themselves as employees and others see them. We generally call this characteristic self-awareness. Here again is the insight to predict how what we say and do will influence others. For example, we should know how what we say will sound from the employees' point of view. Will they resent it, miss the point altogether, or agree with it in principle? Good leaders can often predict the answer accurately. They will even know their own weaknesses and faults and try to compensate for them. They don't let such flaws interfere either with their own performance or with that of their employees. The important thing about seeing ourselves as others see us is that we are more likely to treat others fairly if we know they are reacting to something we have done or said, and especially if we know why they are reacting that way.

Another characteristic of successful supervisors and other leaders that we can acquire is the willingness to work. There are very few substitutes for hard work; for leaders there are none. But the kind of hard work supervisors perform is different from that done by underwriters, coders, and claim adjusters. Leaders are willing to put in long hours on jobs that may not be exciting or rewarding—that may even be unpleasant—just to get the job done. This doesn't mean that they don't know how to delegate; it means that they don't shrink or retreat from those tasks that sooner or later have to be done. When they see that a particular thing has to be done and that it's their job to do it, they tackle it directly, without thinking about getting out of it or putting it off. Of all the characteristics of a successful leader, this may be the most difficult to learn and to master.

Still another common characteristic of successful supervisors is their ability to generate enthusiasm among their employees. This is believable enthusiasm which projects itself from the leaders and catches on with the technical and clerical staff. They, too, seem to be caught up in this willingness to work primarily for the sake of getting the task done. This ability to generate enthusiasm is expressed differently in different leaders, but the results are quickly identifiable. Their people tackle their jobs with interest and excitement, getting satisfaction from their jobs rather than thinking of their work as "that drab interlude between weekends." As we said, leaders may differ in how they project this enthusiasm, but the achievement of the unit or department is there nevertheless. Often the leaders don't have the stereotyped running-around-and-shouting kind of enthusiasm, but it doesn't have to be the continual back-slapping or hand-shaking thing that some people think of as enthusiasm. It can best be described as an intensity that is contagious.

A final common characteristic among good leaders is the willingness to accept responsibility. In fact, such leaders can become bored when there is little or no responsibility connected with what they are doing. They aren't afraid to accept the challenge of doing something that has some risk to it and are willing to take on a job that may allow them to fail, providing it also allows them the opportunity to succeed. They may even go out and look for responsibility if they don't get it otherwise. Instead of waiting for their manager to give them the authority to do something, they will probably be pushing the top of the responsibility ceiling. If they get called on the carpet by their boss, it will probably be for taking on too much responsibility, not too little.

Communicating   In Chapter 5 we discussed in some depth the subject of communication, so we suggest that the reader go back and review the highlights of this subject, this time identifying effective communication as an important characteristic of leadership. However, there are a few points that need to be mentioned here that were not mentioned earlier.

When we get a specific message across to an employee or a group in just the way we want it to get across, that's good communicating. Whether we are writing letters, speaking to groups or individuals, giving orders, or relaying procedures, we haven't ended our responsibilities until the message is received and understood. Whenever we hear ourselves saying, "Don't you remember, I told you . . ." we can be sure we have just indicted ourselves as poor communicators. We have said to the employee or the receiver, "It's your problem, not mine!"

The best way to measure our ability to communicate is to follow up by checking whether what we said produced the results we were trying to get. The usual reason for communicating is to get some kind of action; and the best sign that the message has gotten through successfully is people carrying out the policy, coming in on time, or responding in a way that indicates that they understand what has been said.

One final word about good communicating: it's a requirement of the supervisory job. Supervisors must accept the responsibility for what they communicate; they cannot leave it up to employees and others on the receiving end. They cannot blame their people for not getting the message; they must ensure that their employees get it even if it means doing the communicating all over again. And as important as all the rest, they must work just as hard to communicate up the line as down. Their own managers and other managers up the line ultimately manage according to the quality of the information they get from below.

Motivating Motivation is somewhat different from leadership in that leadership inspires people to work for external reasons—often for the leader—whereas motivation gets them to work for internal reasons. They work because they want to, regardless of how they feel about the boss or the organization. Motivation is probably the single most important aspect of any supervisor's job, because we can't *make* the employees work for very long and expect a good job from them. The lasting, long-term *desire* to work must come from within the individual. Now we have a challenge because it's the specific responsibility of all supervisors to see that employees want to work at their jobs. This means that we can't just say, "Well, it's not my fault. They just don't want to work." If we say that, we are openly admitting we're doing an incomplete job of supervising. We have to accept the responsibility of correcting and improving the motivational "set" of our employees.

In order to motivate our employees, we have to understand why they and other people work in the first place. What is it that makes them work harder or keeps them from working as hard as they can? Of course, the employees have the basic needs for food, clothing, shelter, and safety. But once these needs have been satisfied, our employees still have certain social needs that must be met and are motivated when they see a chance to meet these needs. For instance, they want to be accepted by their fellow employees; they want to think that they are liked and that others want to have them around. In short, they want to be an accepted part of the employee work group. Supervisors must recognize this and make every effort to help their people feel that they are a part of the organization and that the other employees respect their work. We can even do this purposely by relaying any favorable remarks we hear, "By the way, Charlie, the senior underwriter was very pleased that I gave you this agency loss-experience assignment . . ."

Another need employees have is for self-esteem. This relates to what we just said, in that most people like to think that the job they are doing is important and that they are good at it. It's hard for any of us to get motivated over a job that has been downgraded and regarded as not really amounting to much so far as the company or organization is concerned. That's why employees worry about having titles, having their names on the door, or being in the official directory. They like others to know that they are important enough to the organization to be recognized. A little thing, such as putting name plates on the desks, will often go a long way toward meeting these needs. Employees also want to feel that their peers respect them for their ability to do the job and think that what they do is important. They like to think that others look up to them just a little because of their ability. If we come along and disparage or criticize an employee in front of the other workers, we not only embarrass that employee but also can destroy the self-esteem that is so important to him or her. That's the main reason why we should correct in private and approve in public.

In discussing these three points—leading, communicating, and motivating—we haven't meant to imply that we should "baby" employees. It is just good economic sense to recognize that certain things are apt to cause employees to work better and that we should take advantage of these things. In other words, this is a thoughtful effort to get the best results from those who work for us. We expect our employees to care for the equipment and materials we give them. How can we in turn possibly do less for them? It is our approach to getting employees to work effectively because they want to, not because they have to. In the end the results are better for the company or organization, for us as supervisors, and certainly for the employees themselves.

CONTROLLING

While directing is one of the most difficult functions of a supervisor, controlling is perhaps the most critical. When we plan, organize, and direct, there is still the problem of controlling all of what we have planned, organized, and are still directing, because without the proper controls, all the effort may be wasted. Essentially, supervisors control three things or a combination of them—money, material, and people.

Each is handled somewhat differently; each takes a different skill. We find it easier to budget money and materials because they are usually relatively constant. Money will buy just so much, and we have just so much money; so the decision becomes what to do with what we have. But employees aren't that easy to budget; they aren't all alike as are dollars, typewriters, or cars. Even a single individual may show different qualities from one time to another. Typewriters may be identical; employees aren't. Replace one casualty underwriter with another, and things can be quite different. When we start to budget (control) people, we have to take into consideration that they will probably work at a different speed in the morning than they will in the afternoon and that their attitudes and behavior may be a lot different on Monday from those on Friday.

Controlling is most closely related to planning, and this simply says that we must have something to control. Oftentimes we may find ourselves futilely trying to control when we actually don't have a plan to follow. The plan serves as the standard against which we control; so without some kind of plan, we are doing some guesswork with our controlling. How much guesswork can we live with? For example, when we decide in the middle of a semiannual policyholder billing operation that overtime is getting out of hand and we start to "control," we really aren't measuring this against a preset standard (or plan); so it isn't completely correct to say we are practicing the function of control in relation to overtime. If we had planned correctly and started to control overtime as soon as we began our billing procedure, things probably wouldn't have gotten out of hand in the first place. A rule of thumb (which is not really a rule but a guide) says that when we find ourselves in a drastic situation with people, materials, or money, either the planning or the controlling broke down somewhere.

Steps in controlling

We generally think of controlling as having three steps:

1. Determining standards (Example: How much overtime is acceptable in a particular task or operation?)

2. Measuring results against standards (Example: If our actual overtime is 200 hours against a planned maximum of 250 hours and we're only halfway through the project, we have a problem.)

3. Taking remedial action as necessary (Example: Is it possible that employees on overtime need closer supervision? Do they know what they're supposed to do?)

As we have said, the plan in general is the standard, but here we are talking about something more specific. We are looking for the answer to certain basic questions. We need to know who sets the standards and how we will know that they are the standards. The plan may or may not have specified how far from the standards we can go without being in trouble. For example, we can accept an excess of overtime of up to 5 percent over what we planned without getting unduly concerned. That is the kind of information we must have if we hope to control. We might need a daily record of overtime for our unit or department. Another thing we need to know about the standards is who will measure the results of our work and who will see the results of those measurements. Is it our department or branch manager? Is there a quality control person, such as an underwriting analyst, who reports to headquarters? Or do we have someone on our own staff who has the partial responsibility for watching overtime, quality, or some other criterion?

What will be measured is of prime importance. Why are we measuring such things as the number of claim files handled, the number of errors on a computer run, or the number of target dates met on underwriting inspections? Are we getting valid information or are we monitoring a meaningless figure? For example, do we periodically fill out forms that tell the status of our office supply inventory while we short sightedly disregard the heavy economic and morale costs of absenteeism in our unit or department? The point is that if we are not controlling the right things, the controlling effort will not attain cost/benefit for us. Along somewhat the same line, we may find ourselves overcontrolling something. If we have two senior raters assigned to watch for errors or mistakes that junior raters can correct, we are in fact "driving a tack with a sledgehammer." We sometimes discover ourselves overreacting to situations. The manager irately says to watch out for tardiness and we respond by setting up a control system more complicated than is needed. Long after the tardiness, absenteeism, or quality control crisis is past, control forms are still being filled out and reports being sent up the line. Once such forms and reports come into being, it's very difficult to get rid of them, so we should start them only in extreme need, when the expected benefit is in line with the cost in both time and materials.

What are some of the items that we as supervisors may be measuring? Obviously we want to measure the output of such things as bills sent, policies typed, inspections made, and claim files processed. How long did it take? What was the final quality? Then we need to look closely at expenses. When we measure expenses we must measure all of them. Are we taking into account everything that is being charged to the particular job or operation? Are we considering staff help, load factors, and other costs that will eventually have to be accounted for?

We must account for our use of resources. Again we're talking about staff, time, and money, but this time the question of measurement is one of efficient use. Are we doing a good job of matching employees and jobs? It isn't necessarily proof of good supervision if the job gets done well; we must consider who's doing the job. If our employees are capable of doing much more because of experience, education, or natural talent, we can't be too proud of the fact that routine, unchallenging jobs or tasks are done well. The trick is to match ability and job requirements as closely as possible, then allow the employees to grow out of their jobs as they develop. As supervisors we must constantly measure (at least in our minds) how well the employee is matched to the job, as well as whether he or she may have outgrown it and be qualified for a more demanding job.

All of this is true for the other resources we have. Are we really getting the most out of our overtime? Would a good job analysis indicate that we are doing some jobs that should be left undone or eliminated altogether? Are we using overtime to do things that could be done during regular work hours with good time management on our part? We sometimes get trapped by saying that we have to go into overtime to do a very important job, failing to realize that we got into this situation simply because we failed to control properly either our own or our staff's time. We waste valuable time on unimportant things, forcing ourselves and our employees into unnecessary overtime. The same objection applies to using our people on nonessential tasks when they could be doing things that sooner or later must be done. It's all right for everyone to pitch in and help; but if this "pitching in" means that we must neglect other necessary work that will get us behind schedule or cost us time and money later on, then we've made a bad decision.

Using the budget to control

Perhaps one of the oldest and most useful control devices we have is the budget. We often complain about it and even wish we didn't have it, but we should be glad that we have something as demanding as the budget to guide us in our controlling. Very few companies or organizations could run very smoothly without a budget because it gives us a useful standard. It gives us not only something to measure our progress

by, but also something to aim at as an objective or goal. As we periodically compare ourselves with the budget, we also get timely feedback on where we can expect to be at the end of the budget period. It is a way to measure even the small parts of the job, because budgets are made up of parts such as salary and benefits, supplies, equipment, etc. Good budgets consist of accurate parts; bad budgets are made up of padded parts.

This isn't the appropriate place to go into detail on the budget, but let's note several points. It is assembled to let the company, agency, or organization know just how much money there is and where the priority places are. Good budget planning takes into account local needs, and those assembling it will solicit input from all levels in determing the best use of all the money. Trouble can start when each level starts to be unrealistic about its needs, "padding" it a little, so that by the time the total budget is drawn up there is either too big a demand or the organization finds itself looking around for more money than it really needs. Usually when this happens, someone at the top starts to whittle down the figure by a fixed percentage, and everyone down the line gets hurt. "But if I don't raise my figure on estimated overtime I'll get hurt, because top management will probably make an across-the-board cut!" Even if this might happen, that's a management decision, and it doesn't give us and other supervisors the right to pad our estimates just because everyone else does. We shouldn't include anything we can't substantiate or reasonably justify. Sooner or later we will have to account for what we have asked for, and if our figures won't stand that later test, the budget will be cut and our credibility as a supervisor will suffer. The wise thing to do is to make a realistic budget, back it up with realistic estimates and requirements, and then let management wrestle with the problem of cutting it if they have to. Later on, if the work isn't done because of budget problems (lack of money), we can show that we put in a legitimate, realistic request that got cut by someone else.

Measuring results

Once we have determined the standards by which we are to control, we have to measure the results against these standards. Sometimes this measurement is routine—just a matter of seeing how many policies were written, how many automobile claim files were set up, and how many business package policies were sold, and then reporting the obvious results in whatever manner is provided. Not all of our evaluating will be that obvious or that easy. Sometimes we find ourselves in situations where there are so many interrelated, contributing factors that we aren't quite sure just what the results mean. It may be that the overall operation is large and that the end product is the result of the contributions of many people. The ultimate output may be service, and that means we must consider the customer, policyholder, agent, or claimant. How can we measure in circumstances like this?

One good avenue open to us is the process known as sampling. It isn't complicated, but it is a means of getting reliable results about large or complicated operations without measuring every policy, inspection report, or sales trip itinerary and every employee involved. We take a small, average sample and apply the results to the entire unit, department, or branch office. Another way to accomplish the same thing is to analyze one complete operation out of several (such as a commercial property rating unit), assuming that all the rest are like this one. Actually, if we do a pretty good job of sampling, we can get reliable cost-beneficial results. Once we get in the habit, we can increase our sensitivity to ways of getting true samples all of the time. We check the absentee list on random Mondays and Fridays to see if particular employees or a particular number of the staff are absent. We spot-check three or four days in a row to see just how much time our employees are taking for a break or when they are returning from lunch. We look at policyholder or agency complaints once a week for several weeks to see if any one thing is beginning to give trouble.

These things can be good indicators of just how well we are doing, and as such, are practical means of controlling.

When sampling doesn't seem to be an appropriate way of measuring the results, and the measuring of one whole operation or task seems to be too difficult, finding a substitute measurement may help. For example, we can analyze such things as absenteeism or tardiness and get a good idea of the morale in the work unit. If turnover is high, this might be a good substitute measurement of how much orientation or job training is going on. Previous productivity records may be a good indicator of motivation or employee morale, providing other things are equal. The substitute may be a suitable tangible means of measuring intangible things, such as attitudes, job satisfaction, loyalty, etc.

When we are measuring one thing to examine something else, ultimately we'd better be sure our measure is accurate. Even measuring such things as how well one policy typist is doing compared to the others in the office may not give true results. If one typist is doing simple, repetitive, fill-in forms and the others are typing semicustomized policies, counting the number of items or pages might be a poor way of looking at results. On the other hand, one usually accurate policy typist doing the same simple job day-in and day-out may begin to show an unacceptable error rate because the job doesn't have variety in it. The errors may indicate that the typist is getting less job satisfaction than previously. It might be the same for a field claim adjuster. We need to be careful in evaluating one adjuster's results against another's until we are sure the territories and the types of claims are enough alike to be comparable. It's all right to measure the number of claims settled to determine how good an adjuster is providing we know what other claim personnel in the same or similar territories have done. If an incumbent isn't doing as well as he or she should, we need to determine the situation in that territory. Does the claim adjuster know how to adjust fire insurance claims properly? Has he or she had the proper training, the same kind of training as others? In other words, our measurement can be a useful control device only if it is accurate and comparable in all respects. Otherwise it can become an untrustworthy tool to use in making control decisions.

Remedial action

Controlling would be useless if it didn't include the final facet of control—taking remedial action when required. Even though this isn't all of controlling, it certainly includes it. When our measuring processes show that things are running smoothly, we should be confident enough to recognize this and leave things alone. But when the results show that the situation is getting out of hand or that we should be doing better, then we need to know enough to step in and take some corrective action. We may not be the ones to take the action, but we may be the ones to instigate it. As obvious as it seems, merely knowing that something is wrong isn't enough; it is important that we report it to the right person, perhaps the department or branch manager. If we have found that a problem exists somewhere in the group, we should ask ourselves who needs to know about it. It should be someone who has the authority to do something about the situation. Whether it's an overtime problem, a continually late computer run, or what have you, telling the right person as soon as possible may prevent a much more serious problem later on.

When it comes to determining who is this manager or decision-maker, the worst thing we can do is say, "It's not my problem." It is our problem as soon as we hear or know about it, and it's our problem until something is done about it or until someone else takes over the responsibility for the problem. When our manager says, "O.K., I'll take over now," we have done all we can, even if we don't agree with what he or she is doing.

Another important part of notifying the decision-maker is to do it in the right way. That may require more than reporting the bare details in a telephone call made at quitting time. If the receiver shows no evidence of understanding the importance of the problem or misses some of the details, we've got to accept the responsibility for the poor results that come from improper control. If it is feasible, a good approach is to put the problem in writing. This provides a permanent record that we spotted the weakness and made an effort to get it controlled. This latter reason is by far secondary to the first one. If our prime reason for reporting something is just to protect ourselves, we aren't likely to do a thorough job of reporting the facts; neither are we apt to work diligently at organizing our material to ensure that what we say is clear, readable, etc.

Finally, let's reinforce something we said earlier; it's usually better to solve the problem ourselves than to pass it upwards to our manager. This, of course, means we must first have the authority to take the necessary remedial action. It also means we may have to review mentally the planning, organizing, and directing fuctions. Well, if that's what the remedial action requires, being a good supervisor means doing just that, rather than closing our eyes to reality and going blindly ahead toward an eventual result that is wrong or inadequate.

CONCLUSION

There are essentially two parts to planning: planning the work and working the plan. We can't always say which one is more important. We can say only that unless each is done well, the results will suffer. We've seen that getting the work done takes both directing and controlling. We have to emphasize that directing the people under us is well-named; "directing" is the right approach. In many ways, we're neither leading nor pushing our employees, we're pointing the way. Since our ultimate job as supervisors is to see that others do the work, we probably demonstrate our best directing not by dramatic visibility "out in front of the troops" or by giving loud orders, but by motivating, encouraging, and helping others do the work because they want to. The successful supervisors are ultimately the ones who direct by getting their employees to believe in the job, not the boss. (It's all right to believe in the supervisor but that alone shouldn't be the reason they work.) If we seek success at supervising, we have to give up the incorrect notion that only born leaders make good supervisors; we have to understand that supervision is a list of skills performed well, and that each skill can be learned by anyone with ordinary abilities. Directing people is one of those important skills!

Controlling is undramatic but is probably the most critical of the skills required in getting the job done. It's a matter of knowing what's going on and knowing about a problem soon enough and well enough to do something about it before it's too late. It requires faithful attention to details, and disciplined, continued examination of productivity data and records. It means knowing beforehand what we expect from our staff and seeing how close we and they come to those expectations. It means that we have to be flexibile and be able to act quickly to correct a bad situation. It's the last chance we have to correct poor planning and poor directing. If we're adept at it, we might even turn a bad situation into an acceptable one.

EXERCISES

1. Individual exercise: Each person should think of an employee they have working for them now—or have had in the past, or one they know—who is considered to have a poor attitude toward his or her job. They should think of a specific person, not just people in general who have bad attitudes. Thinking of that specific person, they should now decide why they say that person has a bad attitude. Make a list of the reasons.

2. Group activity: Have the group list all the things used to describe the person from Exercise 1 who has a bad attitude. Have the group then decide how many of the things listed are observable and how many of them wouldn't be evident to the observer. (The point of this exercise is to demonstrate that what we consider a "bad attitude" is often poor performance. If that's the case, we try to change the performance rather than the attitude.

3. Individual activity: Let each person select someone they regard highly as a manager and write down the characteristics of that person that explain why he or she was chosen. When this is over, list these characteristics without identifying the managers involved. Note how many of the characteristics were the same. Start to make a list of general characteristics of good managers. Save this list.

4. Individual activity: Let each person think of a great leader they have admired and that they know a little about. These leaders may be from the past—like Napoleon or Lincoln—or they may be from the modern era. After picking a specific person, list the characteristics of that person that made him or her a great leader. When the individuals have completed their list, again summarize this data without listing the names of the leaders. Develop a list of characteristics that great leaders have in common. Save this list.

5. Group activity: Now compare the two lists from Exercises 3 and 4 above. There's a good probability that the lists aren't very similar, though there will be some overlap, of course. From your comparison, decide whether we are looking for the same thing when we talk about a supervisor (or manager) and a "leader." We might go further and ask how some of the leaders we picked would have made out as managers in our organization, especially at the front line of supervision.

6. Group activity: Brainstorm the ways the company or organization has of obtaining information that allows it to "control" the activities of the organization. Which of these are supplied by the first level? Could we, as front-line supervisors, do a better job of supplying this information? Are there any of these control reports or forms that we resist completing or supplying? Why? What might we do or suggest to improve the situation?

8
MOTIVATING
BY ENRICHING THE JOB

Motivation has long been a major subject of discussion among both supervisors and those who train supervisors. Obviously we want our employees to be motivated, for if they are, then they will work harder, be more service-oriented to customers and clients, and enjoy their jobs more. The result will be that they'll get more work done and make our job easier. It's a worthy goal, but it puts a lot of responsibility on motivation and is difficult to reach if we aren't sure how to motivate our people.

WHY DO PEOPLE WORK?

In order to understand how to motivate our staff, it's necessary to find out why people work in the first place. The question actually goes beyond that, because what we really want to know is what gives people the most satisfaction. If we find this out, then we know what makes them work and even what will make them work harder.

Those who have studied the matter in great detail have found out some interesting things about why people work. At first it would seem that everyone works to make money. "Stop paying me and you'll see why I'm working!" someone says, and we almost fall for it until we realize that if we made typists stand up and type all day, they'd probably quit pretty quickly. By this line of reasoning, we'd conclude that people work so they can be reasonably comfortable as they work. We could follow the same line of thinking about benefit plans, treatment from the supervisor, etc. The point is, employees do expect to get paid, they enjoy the things money can bring and they like to make more money. But they don't work just for money.

Primarily, people do what they do to meet certain needs or to get certain satisfactions. They worry about their families' security, so they work to take care of this need. Food, clothing, and shelter are concerns for any employee, so these are strong motivating factors. People also like to be liked. They like to have friends and loved ones who care about them and who show their feelings for them. Often the average employee doesn't expect the job to satisfy this need to any great extent; it is frequently met, in large part, outside the job.

A higher need

Most of us have other needs that can be met largely on the job. In fact, they must be met before the employee is truly motivated. We all like to have our egos "uplifted"; like to think we are useful; like to contribute something for which we alone get the credit. This is a need that comes to the forefront time and again in all of us, and it is the one factor that a supervisor can always depend on to use in motivation.

For a long time managers and supervisors tried to motivate their staffs by making the work location a pleasant place. Often to accomplish this they installed better lighting and effective heating and air conditioning. In many cases music was piped in, and appealing artistic decor was added. Supervisors were specially trained in human relations so they would know exactly how to handle the technicians and clerical staff who worked for them. Supervisors practiced being pleasant to their employees, and many tried extra things like giving time off with pay and excused absences for exceptionally good attendance. Many companies have developed benefits beyond hospitalization and retirement plans. They provide educational assistance for employees who want to continue going to school. Some companies and organizations provide scholarships for the employees or members of their families. Even with all these benefits in addition to attractive wages and vacation plans, the employees may not be motivated to a level which satisfies us.

There is an interesting phenomenon about the benefits mentioned above. If employees in one area or office have them, those who don't have them will be dissatisfied and perhaps even lack motivation. But the presence of such benefits seldom produces motivation over a prolonged period. There is no evidence to show that employees work hard because of a good hospitalization plan; and even when employees get an increase in pay, it rarely motivates them on a permanent basis. Do we then do away with all of these things because they don't motivate employees? Obviously not, because their absence will do a great deal of harm, even if their presence doesn't serve to motivate greatly.

THE KEY TO MOTIVATION

If none of these things motivate people to work hard over a long period of time, what's left for us to do? Actually the answer is simple in principle, although carrying it out is pretty hard. The job itself holds the key to motivation. The job is the one thing that can provide technical or clerical employees with the satisfaction they need to be motivated. They want a chance to succeed. They want recognition for the outstanding job they do; they want to feel that they have a chance to advance; they want to feel that they are making a contribution to the company or organization, whatever their job. All the benefit plans in the world will not, of themselves, provide these satisfactions. Only the work assigned to the employee can do it.

But there is a potential risk here, the job can also prevent these needs from being met. As new supervisors we may fall into the trap that many older ones have experienced—that of failing to use the job as the best means of motivating our workers. In fact, when we take over our assignment from the last supervisor who had it, we may find that the motivating factors have been reduced greatly through lack of skillful supervision. If we just go along doing what our predecessor did, we may miss a great opportunity to provide motivation, get more work done, and impress our manager favorably in the process. Now let's see how it works.

Remember, we are looking for ways in which the employees' desire for recognition, achievement, chance for advancement, etc., can be satisfied right on the job. (We'll see in a minute how some of our staff meet these needs off the job.) We need to look at the total assignment we have given our employees and see what there is about it that will meet these needs. There are several steps we can go through to analyze the job; let's take them one at a time.

First, are jobs clearly defined? Do the employees (and do we) know exactly what is expected of them? Do we have position descriptions or at least task lists? Have we taken the time to go over each detail with each technician or clerk to be sure that he or she understands what is and what isn't his or her responsibility? What about the interfaces between employees or departments? Does each employee know where his or her job stops and someone else's starts? For example, do computer programmers know how their clients or "users" use computer printout? Are there gaps or overlaps in the assignments? Here we're talking about a comprehensive look at the job duties and environment of each individual. Of course some jobs are fairly clearcut and don't require much effort to analyze, but others have some complexities about them that require a careful look to determine exactly where the boundaries are between responsibilities.

Next, we should see if there are any parts of the job that could be done at a lower level because they require less skill than the others do. Are we asking high-priced marketing specialists to type their own reports, underwriters to do miscellaneous filing that file clerks could do, or senior claim adjusters to handle simple claims that are more appropriate for the beginning adjuster? Occasionally some of these tasks may be done best by people with higher job capabilities, but they rarely motivate those employees or give them much of a feeling of accomplishment. The way to approach these situations is to ask ourselves, "Does it really require that person's skill level or talent to do that part of the job?" There are some things in every job that are probably below the competency level of the employee doing it, but the important thing is to see just how much of the total time is spent on these peripheral tasks and how much on those requiring more technical skill, judgment, experience, etc. If the lesser jobs are using up very much of the time, then they should be analyzed and perhaps regrouped and assigned to a junior employee to whom they could be a challenge and an opportunity to grow and learn.

The next step is to look at where an employee's work comes from and where it goes when he or she is through with it. An example would be a filing or records-keeping unit that serves an underwriting department. Too often employees find themselves taking work from some other person or department, doing some operation, then passing it on to someone else. Nowhere in the operation does anyone know what is done with their "work product". Consequently, the sense of real responsibility or accountability diminishes. No one has a sense of being a part of either the beginning or the end of the job or task.

THE SUPERVISOR'S RESPONSIBILITY

We also need to evaluate our own actions in trying to enrich the job. Are we still doing part of the job that should rightly be done by our coders, marketing specialists, or statisticians? If we came to our job from the one below us there is a better-than-average chance that we're still doing more of our old technical job than we should. Just because we're good at it doesn't justify not training someone else to do it. A real test of our supervisory skill is to see if we can quickly divorce ourselves from doing the jobs that others are paid to do and tackle those things that we are paid to do.

It doesn't come easy. We all look for satisfactions in and from our jobs, and since supervision is a tough, demanding job where the responsibilities sometimes aren't clear, we tend to get frustrated. Trying to overcome this frustration often leads us to find satisfaction in working with the technical side of the job instead of with people. This means we may start settling claims, underwriting risks, stuffing envelopes, doing our own filing—and anything to get a little satisfaction of accomplishment. But we should remember that every time we do these things, we are, in effect admitting a little bit of failure. We're trying to enrich our jobs at the expense of our technical and clerical staff who should be doing these things.

Supervisors have to look for things that will enrich the jobs under them, even if it means reorganizing the work or shifting responsibilities. They have to recognize that not every job in the department or unit can be enriched, and that not every employee can accept an equal amount of responsibility. Each employee must first earn the right to whatever responsibility is added to his or her job. Too often we confuse the process and give additional responsibility before employees have shown a willingness to accept it. We naively imagine that our doing this will motivate them, but under these circumstances they may see our action as increasing their work rather than their responsibility. We do better to reward the acceptance of responsibility. Note the difference between the following two approaches:

"John, up until now I've been handling this loss-ratio analysis. From now on I'm making it your responsibility."

"John, since you've been making the decisions on analyzing loss ratios—and I've just been signing off on it—from now on would you like to send it out directly without my looking at it?"

In the first case it sounds like more work, even a little bit of a threat. In the second case it comes out as a reward for achievement, a recognition of acceptable performance, and an improved opportunity for John to show us what he can do.

AVOID "MORE WORK"

One reason for rewarding acceptable performance is that when we begin to analyze and reorganize the work, we are apt to base it on each employee's capabilities, rather than according to our plans and ideas. The problem can come when we look at a job and say, "I need to give this computer programmer more responsibility," then assign more of the same kind of work he or she is already doing. What we have done is enlarged or expanded the job, not enriched it. (Having to dig a wider or longer ditch is not apt to motivate as much as selecting where it should be dug.)

PROTECT MOTIVATION

Strangely, if we try to motivate our employees by giving them more responsibility, we may find that we have left ourselves open for criticism. For example, suppose that Linda our customer relations representative, does a great job of answering certain types of inquiries from policyholders or agents. Both her judgment and her knowledge of our renewal procedures are excellent. We realize that she is checking with us only as a matter of routine. She makes the right decision, clears it with us, then handles the matter to completion. But there are times we are out of the department or office, and action stops until we are able to give our approval.

Here is a perfect opportunity to consider enriching her job. We know she has earned the right to make her own decisions and to handle the matter without our being involved, so we could offer her the recognition of doing the entire thing without our approval. If she agrees, all indications point to her doing an even better job because it really is her job now.

Now a problem can arise. Unless our manager is in agreement with what we are doing, we could be misunderstood. Everything is fine as long as Linda makes the right decision. But what happens when something is done that is wrong or contrary to policy? When we are called in by our boss to explain the action and reason for the error, we have a choice of blaming Linda or accepting the blame ourselves. It may not be enough to say, "I was trying to motivate her," because an obvious question is, "Why does she need motivating? I though she was a good employee."

It's just as bad to say, "I've been letting her make those decisions because when I'm out of the office, there's no one to give the approval." The response to that might be, "Maybe you're falling down on your job by being away too much." The point is that there can be some risks involved in giving recognition to employees who have demonstrated their ability to achieve. We must be sure that our manager is aware of the principles involved and agrees to go along with our efforts. The worst result would be for our boss to say, "This nearly got us into trouble, so from now on I want you to check how we handle our customer inquiries." By the same reasoning, our manager could probably justify checking everything he or she does and so on up the line. Once such edicts are issued, they are difficult to remove or to change.

PRODUCTIVITY-MINDED MANAGEMENT

We've spent much time talking about motivating our employees, enriching their jobs and our own, and the responsibility we have as supervisors to do these things; but it wouldn't be right to leave a chapter on motivation without commenting on productivity. When it comes right down to it, getting out the work or providing the service is what it's all about. It's ultimately why there are employees and why there are supervisors. For the most part, even charitable organizations don't exist just to keep the employees on the payroll. Hospitals and service organizations have to give good service; they have to think about saving money. Profit-centered organizations understand this at management levels, but it may not be understood at front-line supervisory levels. First-line supervisors may be so closely tied to the working unit that they miss the point that productivity is the reason there is any profit at all.

We have to understand that "saving money" and "making a profit" aren't bad words. They are good reasons for working effectively. Whatever style the supervisor finally develops as his or her own, it must take into account that something will have to be done if the employees don't produce (whatever the reason). This doesn't suggest that we are indifferent to the employee and that we don't try hard to provide means of motivation. In fact, it means the opposite. We do all of these things because we've seen that they produce motivated employees and that a motivated staff is apt to produce more. It does suggest that the supervisor must realize that just making the employee happy on the job or making the organization a good place to work isn't the end of the matter. Our employees should understand this, too. The end result is to get the most production from the fewest employees while offering a quality product or service. In a profit-making organization, like a company or agency, it also means producing it better and/or cheaper than the competition.

What, then, do we do as a result of this knowledge of the need for productivity? We certainly monitor both the quantity and the quality of the results in terms of productivity. If we believe that employees are likely to respond with productivity when they believe in the job, then we do whatever we can to enrich their jobs to make them meaningful and to demonstrate how their job contributes to the overall result. We'll monitor production figures and job standards to see if we're on target; we'll see how many inspections our loss-prevention specialists are making; we'll monitor how many auto liability claim cases are handled by our adjusters; we'll see how many pages of error-free typing are produced; we'll see how many policyholders or agents phone in complaints. Then we'll communicate this information to employees as the basic reason for their being employed, and we'll also communicate our dissatisfaction when the unit continually falls short of the objectives and goals that are reasonable.

Finally, we must recognize that the first-line supervisor can be more sensitive than anyone else in the company or organization to the major causes of inflation and the means of helping control it. To see this, we review the typical inflationary pattern within a company or agency:

Wages increase.

Cost of materials and services increases.

Time to produce a product like an insurance policy or provide a service remains the same or increases.

Production of product or service increases slightly or not at all.

When these four elements or conditions exist—and it may not require all four of them—we have cost inflation within our organization. That means we have to pay more for the same amount of productivity or service. In turn, this can mean our employees are concerned about a salary increase. And that can mean it's going to cost our employer more to provide the same service or product to policyholders, claimants or agents—so rates and premiums will have to be raised, and the spiral will continue. It will tend to continue under these circumstances until productivity goes up far enough to offset the increased costs. If we get more production for the same amount of dollars or other resources, we can even lower the price and the users of the service or product can get more for their money instead of less. This is one way to neutralize the effects of inflation within our organization. The new supervisor, especially at the first level, has to think continually of ways to get more productivity from the same employees or to get the same production at lower cost, or both. An alternative could be to improve the product or service so that when the customer pays more, he or she gets more for the money. An example would be offering higher dollar limits of liability to a policyholder for the same or less money, but this may prove to be an impractical alternative to controlling the cost of a product or service that has already proven satisfactory.

CONCLUSION

As we suggested in the last chapter, when we were talking about directing people, leadership in the world of supervision can be different from the rest of the world's idea of leadership. So is motivation. Many think that motivating people means stirring them up to where they go charging out and work themselves into exhaustion just because their leader has inspired them so much. In supervision, the real goal is to get them involved in fulfilling enough of their own needs through facets of the job to get satisfaction from doing the job. When the job is challenging and meaningful enough, and gives enough recognition, the supervisor is motivating the employee in a practical way. The supervisors' job is to make sure the job offers all or many of those characteristics. There's not much that will motivate an employee more than having responsibility for some specific tasks that are well-defined and recognized as necessary to the organization. Not everyone deserves or can take responsibility, and it should be given as a reward only when those it's offered to agree to take the consequences of failure as well as the rewards of success. This means that in addition to having the right to be right, the employees must have the right to make mistakes and to be wrong. If employees know they will have to live with the consequences of their mistakes, the end result is employees who work much harder at being right and who are, in fact, motivated.

EXERCISES

1. Individual activity: Let all participants think about themselves in their present jobs. Each should write down what events or happenings make an effective day for him or her right now. Think of two or three situations in the last week where motivation has been high—high enough that the employee has thought about the activity before coming to work and was anxious to get to work and get into it. After all have listed several situations, let them go back and analyze each one and see what it was that made the job exciting or motivating for them. Think of the characteristics of the job, not the actual activity. When all have finished, record the information for future use.

2. Group discussion: Looking at the list from Exercise 1 above, decide how many of these items could be built into any job whether technical or clerical. See how many of the factors were common with everyone. Is it possible that we could motivate our employees with the same kinds of things?

3. Individual activity: Let each person think of one employee who is usually very motivated to do the job assigned. Carefully analyze the job or task that employee is doing, and the way we make the assignment. See if we can determine just what it is that motivates the employee on the job. Is it possible that something about the job motivates the employee, rather than his or her own attitude. (It's not enough just to say, "Anything I ask that employee to do makes him or her excited." We also have to see how much responsibility we've given the person, and how we make the assignment.) Record the results of the group, and save the information for further use.

4. Group activity: Analyze the "motivation factors" given in the last exercise. Are there any common factors? Would any of them motivate us? Are they similar to the ones found in Exercises 1 and 2? Now the critical question: Would the same approach work for all of our employees, technical or clerical?

5. Individual activity: Let each person think of one employee who usually is not motivated much at all. Carefully analyze the job or task the employee is doing and the way we make assignments to him or her. See if we can determine if there is anything about the job that fails to motivate the person. Is it possible that the job or parts of it aren't very motivating? Record the group's results and save for future use.

6. Group activity: Analyze the characteristics given in Exercise 5. Throw out the ones that are not measurable, like "The employee is just lazy," and deal only with those that have to do with the nature of the job or the way the assignment is given. See if there is anything about the job that fails to motivate. If we were working for this supervisor and had this job or task to do, and had this amount of responsibility, would we be motivated?

9
INTERVIEWING SKILLS

When we talk with our employees about specific things, such as discussing how they are doing, correcting some deficiency in their work performance, or trying to assist them in solving some personal problem they may have, we call this "interviewing." This is one more technique we, as a new supervisor, need to learn; and the more we do it the more effective we should get at it. The problem is that we don't do very much interviewing from day to day, so even experienced supervisors can get rusty. The best approach is to look at the techniques required, practice them whenever we can, think through each interview beforehand, and brush up on the techniques each time we have another interview.

In this chapter we will first talk about the general principles of interviewing, then look at some specific kinds, namely Employment, Appraisal, Counseling, Disciplinary, and Exit. As we said, interviewing is usually not an everyday occurrence for the supervisor, so we can't expect to become instant experts. However, since there are some basic points we can remember, it's good to study them. We identify and describe them so we can talk about them separately, but in practice we may sometimes find ourselves combining them.

GENERAL PRINCIPLES

Basically there are three general purposes of an interview: (1) to predict behavior, as in the case of an employment interview where we want to know how well we think the employee or potential employee will do in a particular job; (2) to change behavior where it isn't meeting a standard, such as the disciplinary interview when an employee is tardy, performs below production standard, or displays an attitude that has a negative effect on the behavior of others; (3) to establish exactly what the behavior is, as in the appraisal interview. When we are preparing for an interview—and let's remember to prepare before we have one—we need to decide which purpose we have in mind. We need to know why are we having it, why are we having it now, and why are we having it with this particular employee. Further, we need to establish not only why we are doing this, but also what we hope to accomplish in the interview. If the purpose or objective is to change behavior, we must know what specific behavior we want. A vague dissatisfaction with the employee's performance is not enough to go on. It's embarrassing to tell the technical or clerical staffer, "I don't like the way you're doing it now, but I can't specify what I'd like you to be doing." Once we've pinpointed what we don't like and what we would prefer as an alternative, we need to know how we are going to get the employee to change. And we should know whether we expect the total change to be made as a result of this interview or whether change will demand additional steps later.

The best thing to do before an interview is write out these key points on paper. We don't need to be elaborate. We simply write ourselves a note stating the purpose of the interview, where we're going, why we're going there, and how we expect to get there—all of which forces us to organize our thoughts. This may ultimately convince us that this is not the time to have the interview, that we need to talk to all of our staff, that we need more information, or that we probably should have had the interview earlier. At the least it will give us an opportunity to spend a few helpful moments analyzing the situation before we get into it.

Establishing the proper climate

Let's reemphasize something we said earlier: Interviewing is talking with employees or prospective employees. We didn't say talking *to* them or talking *at* them, we said talking *with* them. There is a difference. Talking with people means that we listen as much as we talk. It means that the employee or applicant has something to say and a right to say it. When the interview is over, we can be sure it was a poor one if our reflections tell us that we did most of the talking. This probably indicates that we did the talking and he or she did the listening. On the other hand, we can probably say that it was a good interview if we got a lot of information and the employee did at least half of the talking. Listening is one thing we must determine to do.

We must also determine to be fair. We must face up to the fact that each of us probably has prejudices that affect our thinking. Since we each see things from our own standpoint, we most likely don't see them alike. Part of deciding to be fair in our interviews is to admit that there is always the chance that the employees might be right. At least there is the possibility that they could be more right than we are. This doesn't mean that we go against the established facts. It simply means we admit that our employees have some right on their side and we are willing to hear them out. One good way to approach the interview is to imagine ourselves in the interviewees' position and view the situation from their standpoint, even if we think the situation is an extreme one. Another facet of fairness is deciding how we will let interviewees know we want to be fair. A convincing way is to show them, not tell them. When people say something, we listen and accept what is said. We refer to it later, to let them know that we listened. We give them a chance to defend themselves, to state more facts, or to disagree with us, all in a threat-free climate.

We start our interviews by letting the interviewees know that we want to talk to them under the best conditions. When they come in we greet them in such a manner as to let them know we were expecting them and we are planning to listen and talk. We don't say, "Wait a few minutes until I finish reviewing this claim file and I'll talk to you," nor do we just acknowledge their presence and keep on working. Either way tells the interviewees that they come second, at best. That's not polite, and it's not the impression we want to create. Instead we greet them and demonstrate that they come first by making sure that our phone calls are taken by someone else and that no one will interrupt us. We seat our interviewees comfortably, not in an awkward position where they have to turn to see us or otherwise be uncomfortable. If we have room or it isn't too obvious that we don't usually do it, it's a good idea to come out from behind our own desk and sit beside our interviewees rather than across the desk from them. Of course, if we have papers and notes we need to refer to, then sitting behind the desk is probably the best arrangement.

Any time we are talking with people, it makes good sense to open the conversation on some light topic instead of jumping right to the point. Our opening remarks show an interest in our interviewees, their families, their jobs, or their hobbies. This should be genuine, not forced and not too long. Interviewees know we want to talk to them and they may even know what we want to talk about. Some supervisors like to sneak into the subject, but that is a risky way to get to the point because we shouldn't have anything to hide. Remember we wanted to talk to each of these people, so we have provided the opportunity for the interview. Even if they asked for these sessions, we still shouldn't wait for them to bring up the subject. We are the supervisor and we are in *our* office or at our desk. It's up to us to take the lead. So, as soon as appropriate, we start talking about the subject of the interview without beating around the bush. "Jim, I called you in so we could go over your question about the agency loss ratios . . ." This gets us started and no one is surprised. This way Jim knows quickly what the subject is about and can get his thoughts in order. He knows why he's there and what we expect him to discuss, and he can give us information without guessing. After all, we want him to be free to speak and to give us as much good, usable information as possible. This can happen only if he knows what it is we're talking about.

As we have said, the interview is as much listening as talking. We give full attention to the answers to our questions; we listen when the interviewees talk. We consider their remarks, answer their questions the best we can, but keep the interview focused on the topic at hand. One error often committed is to let those being interviewed get us off the subject and cause us to discuss irrelevant things that we really aren't prepared to talk about. When our time is up we may discover that we haven't reached the interview objective and that we either have to schedule another interview or extend this one longer than we intended. If we have directed the interview properly, we should close without letting it drag on. Once we've gotten the information we wanted, answered the interviewees' questions, or settled the problem, the wise thing to do is to end the session as quickly and politely as possible. One good way for us to close and also get a little feedback from them is to ask them to sum up the findings as they see them. This way we can see if they have any misunderstandings about the things that have been discussed and also let them know that the interview is over. If there is any follow-up action to be taken, state that plainly as well as who will do the action:

"I'll call you Thursday on these premium billings."

"We'll try this new coding procedure for a month, then talk again."

"You call me when you've decided what you want to do about the limits of liability for that policy."

We should remember to let the interviewees leave on the same friendly note they came on, regardless of the outcome of the interview. Even if there is a disagreement, there is no need to be disagreeable.

THE EMPLOYMENT INTERVIEW

Often the job of interviewing new or prospective employees is not the sole responsibility of the new supervisor, but it's well to know some of the techniques just the same. Even if the personnel department or our manager makes the ultimate decision on whom to hire, we still may have to interview the individual to decide exact job placement or to give our recommendation. If there is a possibility that the individual will end up working for us, we should not try to avoid or sidestep the interview. Let's examine why this interview is so important to us, the individual, and the organization.

Any time we add someone to our unit or department, we are in the process of trying to match a person and a job. Surely, few things we do can affect the outcome of the job more than this. There is a good chance that we are starting someone on an insurance career; we are saying that this person has the unique qualifications to fit the particular job, or at least the potential to grow into it. In a real way the individual is relying on us to decide whether or not he or she is suited to the job. When we ask the typical questions so often asked: "Well, do you think you will fit into health insurance underwriting?" or, "How do you think you will like statistical analysis?" we may be asking unfair questions. If we've done our interview correctly, we are in a better position than the applicant to know the answers. We know the job and we should know him or her pretty well by now. All of these are reasons why the interview is important from the applicant's standpoint.

From the organization's standpoint it's equally important to match the person and the job. It's usually easier to get an employee onto the payroll than off it. It's much more enjoyable too! So we should do the hiring carefully and thoughtfully. Sometimes the organization may pass employees around from one job or office to another, trying in vain to find something they can do. In all probability they shouldn't have been hired in the first place. Whoever made the mistake in hiring them has cost our organization considerable money, wasted time, and frustration. We must do our job of interviewing carefully so this can't be said about us a few years from now. Finally, we need to do a good job of selecting the new employees who are going to work for us because they are going to be doing at least a part of our work for us; and if they don't work out well, we aren't likely to be able to reach our supervisory objectives.

When we conduct employment interviews we should be certain of their purpose. Primarily, there are two basic objectives we want to accomplish—give information and get information. Perhaps getting information is the most important. What kind of information do we want to get? First, we want to get past-employment history, particularly in insurance. We need to find out what skills our prospective employees have actually used, not just which ones they have. How much growth have they shown? What kind of promotions or advancement did they have on their last job? How stable are they as employees? Does this applicant have a record of moving from one job to another or has he or she been on one or two for several years? Such questions as, "What did you do to develop in your last assignment as a statistician?" can tell us a lot if we listen carefully enough.

Asking questions is a good way to find out about the interviewees' attitudes toward supervision, too. Is this one aggressive, not wanting to be supervised? Is that one easily disgruntled? Adaptable? "What kind of manager do you like best?" "Tell me about some of the effective supervisors you have worked for?" "What bothers you the most about managers you have known?" These aren't trick questions, the answers should give us useful information. We aren't playing games, and we should let interviewees know that. If an applicant for a claim adjuster's job says she likes supervisors who let her alone and let her make mistakes as well as get credit for what is good, then she may have the makings of an excellent employee. If another says he likes a boss to give him minutely specific directions on how to appoint agents and keep him continually posted along the way, we may find that he isn't as aggressive as we would like, especially if the job is one that may require individual thinking. And if still others tell us a woeful series of stories about supervisors who didn't understand them or who picked on them all the time, we may find that within two or three months we'll fall into that same category—hearing complaints about how we pick on them!

At this time it's wise for us to explore the personal ambitions of employees. Where do they expect to go in the company or organization? (Not what specific job, since they may not know our organization that well, but how high up either in a technical or supervisory job do they feel their capacity for responsibility and authority might take them?) We need to know whether they're going to be willing to learn the jobs in a job family one at a time, or whether they expect to move up rapidly without really finding out what's going on along the way. We should try to learn whether they will be content to work satisfactorily on one job without a promise of promotion. But we don't find out these things by just asking them. We don't baldly say, "Do you want to learn the computer programming job before moving up?" We can ask the interviewees just how they see themselves preparing for a career or what part they think experience plays in their development. Here again, we aren't likely to get explicit answers but we can get some good indicators. Our ability to interpret the answers will grow as we get more experience, but it isn't as hard as it might sound. The key is our ability to listen.

The second major purpose of the employment interview is to give information to the applicant. Though they don't need to know everything right then, prospective employees do need to know something about the company or organization. They need to know about those policies, objectives, procedures, rules, and benefits that most affect them and apply to them. Merit salary increases and paid vacations probably mean much more to the young single applicant than the sickness benefits and the retirement plan. Accomplishments of the organization, provisions for the family, and promotion opportunities mean much to the mature person looking for a career. This isn't the place to oversell the organization. We neither have to accentuate the weaknesses, nor pretend the company or the job is perfect. Above all, be honest, especially if interviewees ask such specific questions as whether overtime might be required, heavy travel is involved, or attendance at a home-office training course is necessary. It's better for them to know about any requirements and demands now than to find them out later by surprise.

Part of the reason for giving out information is to let applicants know about the job they will be doing. Again, honesty is the rule. If there is likely to be sustained deadline pressure, say so. If the job has some routine aspects, don't be afraid to mention it but at the same time point out the more exciting features as well. If inexperienced interviewees aren't likely to understand insurance terminology, don't spend a lot of time going into great detail about the job. Let them ask questions after you have given them enough information to make their questions meaningful. It's a good idea even to "help" them ask questions. "Do you have any questions about the billing operation?" "Is there something in the marketing specialist's job that I can give you more information about?" A key consideration here is to be sure not to hire a person on the next job above the one he or she will be working on. To tell interviewees "After a little while you should be promoted to computer programmer and on that job you will be doing , . . " is a poor approach. If they won't take the entry-level job we are offering them, don't promise them a higher-level one as a bribe to take this one! Above all, let them know what their salary and vacation schedules are.

Make it clear to them in exact terms. It can be good to give interviewees a rough breakdown of the deductions so they won't be surprised if their check is less than they expected. If they aren't entitled to a full vacation with pay the first year, be sure they know it. Don't rationalize by saying they didn't ask about that. Don't leave it up to them to ask about such important considerations.

If interviewees ask about the future, we tell them to the best of our ability; but obviously we shouldn't promise them anything that we aren't sure we can deliver. Perhaps the best thing to do is let them see what others with backgrounds and experience similar to theirs have done. But since it's an interview, it's well to get their views, their ideas, their questions about the future. Find out where they see themselves going and how fast they want to get there. "Where do you think your skills and talents will best direct you in the life (or the casualty) end of the business?" This kind of question will always give us some insight into the interviewees' hopes and aspirations. They must realize that the future depends as much on them as on the company or organization, so questions that will let us know how they are likely to relate to the organization and the people around them will give us more information. The questions should be worded correctly, though, or the answers won't give very meaningful information. It would be useless to ask, "How did you get along with your last supervisor?" Anybody would be foolish to answer anything but, "Fine!" As we have already suggested, if we ask, "What kind of manager or teacher did you like the most?" we get the employees' views, not a baited answer. The same is true about asking, "Do you get along with people?" That's what we want to know, but we won't find out by asking the direct question. We'll get better information if we say something like, "Tell me about some of the underwriters you liked or disliked on your last job." This is a leading question; but since we haven't supplied the interviewees with any clues as to the "right" answer, they must answer from their own ideas and feelings.

Government impact on the employment interview

Federal and state legislation, court decisions, and administrative rulings together have affected the structure and procedure of the employment interview.

At the federal level, for example, Title VII of the Civil Rights Act of 1964, as amended in 1972, broadly applies to hiring, job assignments, promotions, and many other factors. Basically, the Act prohibits discrimination in terms, conditions, or privileges of employment on the basis of race, color, national origin, sex, and religion.

Similar federal and state legislation prohibits discrimination because of age, physical handicaps, and other factors. Governmental agencies are empowered to enforce these various acts.

Our immediate concern is the impact that this legislation, court rulings, and other decisions have on the employment interview. In brief, questions asked by the supervisor or interviewer should be relevant—that is, they should pertain to whether or not the applicant can actually or potentially do the job in question.

Questions that don't support this criterion of relevancy shouldn't be asked. For example, if the job requires that the applicant use their own car, then we may ask whether they own a car; if the job doesn't require this, then the question shouldn't be asked.

PLANNING THE INTERVIEW

Planning the interview can ensure that we ask the right questions. First, before the interview we review the position guide or position description, performance standards, and required or desirable personal qualifications. Next, we decide the type of questions we'll ask in order to determine whether the applicant meets the job criteria we identified earlier. We scan the application blank before the interview, noting areas such as work experience on which we'll need more information. As far as possible, we outline, at least generally, the flow of questioning as we would desire it to go.

Beyond this, it's basically a matter of preparing for the interview with attention to key universal elements: place—comfortable and private; time—adequate and undisturbed; objective(s)—clearly understood; materials or forms needed—at hand and reviewed beforehand.

Rather than list questions that we can and cannot ask—a list that will probably be out of date quickly because of continuing legislative, judicial, and administrative actions—we advise the line supervisor or manager to seek specific staff assistance on this and other aspects of equal employment opportunity. The first source should be the personnel department within the company or organization.

Some outside sources of help would be books and articles on the subject; short courses and seminars sponsored by colleges, universities, and industry and other trade associations; and consultation with governmental directives and administrative rulings.

THE APPRAISAL INTERVIEW

When we appraise our employees, we should include an interview to discuss the matter with them. This is called an appraisal interview. It
should be done periodically for the benefit of both the employees and
ourselves. They need to know their strengths and weaknesses, and we
need to know how they see themselves and the job. But if the company
or organization has a regularly scheduled time for making appraisals, we
must be careful not to wait until that one certain time each year to let
employees know how they're doing. If we expect smooth development
of the people who work for us, we must let them know as often as
possible where they need to grow. Once a year isn't enough. So the
appraisal interview isn't something that's done once a year to satisfy
some organizational policy; it's something that we do with our employees to discuss their growth and development.

The primary purpose of the appraisal interview is to assess how employees contribute to the organization now and how they will fit into it
in the future. It should be one of the more welcome interviews we
have with the employees, because it's a time to do what we should
spend time doing—helping employees grow. For this reason we
shouldn't confuse this type of interview with the disciplinary one
to be described later. This isn't the time to focus on only the faults of
the interviewees; we don't save up the disciplinary infractions to bring
them out at this time. The purpose of the appraisal interview should be
clear in our minds and clear to the employees. They should know why
we're having the dialogue and make plans for their own inputs to the
interview.

Employee participation

Employees should be given every chance to be a part of every interview,
especially this one. They should know well in advance that the interview is planned. They should know beforehand that we want them to
participate and that we will be discussing the future as well as the past.
Of course, each interview starts with putting the employee at ease, but
this one shouldn't take as long as the others. Most employees want to
know how well we think they are doing and are anxious to get to the
subject, especially if they know in advance that we want to talk about
their progress. The first thing we should do on getting into the subject
is to let the employees tell us how they see themselves. And it's good if
at this same time we also allow them to explain how they see their jobs.

Through a brief oral summary they let us know what they think their job is. This may explain why they have certain shortcomings, because there may be some things they just don't know they're supposed to do. As we begin to compare our views with those of the interviewees, we need to be careful that they don't lose sight of the fact that we want them to be a part of the discussion. If we become too dominant, they could begin to think that it doesn't really make much difference what they think and that we already have our minds made up, so we try to keep them in the conversation throughout the entire interview. We give them the honest impression that this is their session, their opportunity to get the facts on how they're doing and where they're going. When they see something differently from the way we see it, their opinion should be treated with respect. If they have the supporting data, then we should accept what they say. (Just because they work for us doesn't mean that they have less mental ability or are less honest.)

In the appraisal interview we should give the future its due. Even when we're talking about past performance, we want it to relate to the employees' future performance. How can they increase their efficiency? What are they doing now—such as on-the-job training—that is likely to enhance their chances for promotion in the future? As much as possible, we should let them set their own performance improvement objectives and decide what actions will produce the best results for them and the organization. Certainly they should be allowed to participate in discussing any corrective action that is decided on. As we look at the interviewees' future, we help them set both long- and short-range goals for themselves. The long-range ones might deal with their ambitions, their study, and their direction in the organization, such as marketing, operations, supervision, etc. The short-range ones will have to do only with the job at hand. We will want to caution them that there is a certain amount of risk in looking too far ahead, especially if they begin to forget about the obligations of their present job. Too many employees have lost the future because they didn't give enough attention to the present. Part of our obligation as a supervisor is to let the employees under us know how they are doing on their present assignment so they will have an opportunity to make the most of the future. The appraisal interview allows us an excellent opportunity to do this, especially if we let the employees be a part of setting both the short- and the long-range objectives for themselves.

As in any interview, we should be sure the employees know exactly what we are saying. We should state how we see their job and their future. As their interview draws to a close, we should begin to summarize and clear up any misunderstandings that have arisen. If we have decided upon some specific training or other course of action, we should also state that clearly. If there is to be some kind of follow-up, then the time and place should be settled, preferably in writing. Even if another meeting isn't scheduled, we should establish that we don't want to wait until next year to talk about the interviewee's progress and future. Not only should employees feel free to talk to us, but they should be equally free to initiate such a meeting.

Finally, we should note that some employees may not accept the things we say and may take our appraisal efforts as just another chance to criticize them. They may not agree with our estimate of them, and may rationalize and blame the organization or other people around them. If we do our best and the situation still turns out this way, then we have found out even more about these employees than we already knew. We now know that they can't take criticism and that they lack the ability to see themselves as others see them. If so, then so be it. We've done our part; we'll continue to do our part. We'll continue to let these employees participate in forming their future. We'll continue to let them participate in these types of interviews. And we'll even look critically at our own information to see if it's faulty in some way. But we must still be the supervisor, and we must still hold to that which we see and believe. Though it probably won't be a real problem, the worst thing we can do is to let employees bluff us into changing our minds or

our actions. As we have said, employees want us to tell them how we see them both in the job now and in the future. If we have done a good job of preparing for the interview, we'll be glad we conducted it, and will look forward to the next one!

THE COUNSELING INTERVIEW

Sometimes our technical and clerical employees have problems, and the result is that we find ourselves involved in counseling interviews. Since the problems may be of the emotional type, these interviews will differ from the others we will have. Even the approach will be different. Most often, counseling interviews come about as a result of employees coming to us, rather than our going to them. Because of this we can be perceived in a different light. We don't have the same kind of controls on the time or duration or on the topics to be discussed, as we do in the other types of interviews. Of course, as supervisors we are concerned about the employees' well-being; but we are also concerned with their performance. If their problems affect their performance on the job, we must try to help them resolve those problems in a way to protect the individual as well as the company or organization. Many personal problems are not job-related, but if they have a negative effect on job performance, most employees will realize it. They'll know that they aren't doing as well as they are capable of doing, and this can compound their worries, making the original problem worse. For this reason, if it is possible, we should try to be sympathetic to our employees when they bring up personal problems. Maybe all we can do is to listen patiently but in some cases we may be able to refer them to the personnel department or to professional counseling resources within the organization or in the community. This in itself may make them feel a little better and more capable of dealing with other things.

Interestingly enough, employees may not even know the real causes of their problems. They may have some family problems that cause them to come to work in a bad frame of mind, to interpret things in the wrong light, or even to say and do things that create problems for others around them. They may have financial problems that cause them to worry and fail to concentrate on their job, which in turn may create errors or cut into production schedules. It may cause mistakes that show up later downstream in our operation. One of the serious consequences of employees' worrying about financial problems may be that they misunderstand what their salary should be and what kind of time intervals they should have between raises.

Help them out

Because of the personal nature of these interviews and the fact that the employees have to come to us, we have to be very careful to treat the interviews as opportunities to help them, not threaten them. We shouldn't start with, "I'm glad you're here. I've been wanting to talk to you." This would probably turn the employee off. The best thing to do is simply let them know we will let them talk and will listen to what they say. We also want to convey the idea that we want to help. Because the employee has come to us, this is a good opportunity to get things straightened out; but we have to be careful not to go beyond our capabilities. Remember, we are not trained psychologists! If we think we can help, we should do our best to help. If we have any doubt, we should quickly refer the employee to someone who is better trained than we are to do the counseling.

As we listen to our employees and try to decide what advice to give them, we need to face the fact that we may never get either full or accurate information from them. We may get false conclusions based on too little information, emotion or imagination. Because of this, we must be careful not to repeat the same mistakes by drawing hasty conclusions. The worst thing we can do is to form an opinion very early in the interview, then look only at that evidence which supports our opinion. However, this doesn't mean that we can't recommend any action or make any suggestions. It's possible to help employees even without getting all the information we'd like. The fact that they don't go away with all their problems solved doesn't mean that their meeting was unsatisfactory. If we have provided them with the opportunity to unwind, to talk or to realize that someone will actually listen and not try to regulate them, we may have helped them to put their mind at ease. If they attack the organization or policies, we should answer their questions truthfully but avoid being defensive. We want to keep from getting emotional, especially if an employee is that way. We don't want to avoid the truth about the organization, an employee's work, or our feelings toward him or her. We could do more harm than good if we tell an employee that everything is rosy, knowing all the time that we are going to have to take some serious disciplinary action in the near future.

Our best and most practical approach is to let the employee take the ultimate responsibility. We listen. We ask questions. We make some suggestions, if appropriate. Often the employee shows that he or she has the strength to face the problem but wants a sympathetic ear. In such a case, we could do a lot of harm if we took over. All of us like to have someone to talk to now and then, even though we aren't necessarily looking for advice or expecting the person we're talking with to agree or disagree with us. We just find that we understand our problem at the end of the conversation, and even more so if the other party happens to ask us a pertinent question or two. So it is when an employee comes to us with a problem and appears to just want to talk. Our best response is to let him or her do just that.

Even if we mistakenly start off by taking over, we should immediately begin to look for ways to return the ultimate responsibility to the employees. Gradually we shift it back by asking questions and letting them supply the answers instead of the other way around. As they begin to take the responsibility again, we keep them on the right track by asking the right questions—questions that simply make them face another truth or help them avoid the wrong conclusion—and step in only when they appear to be running out of steam. We should avoid trying to be the hero and get all the credit for the solution. We're probably looking for the credit without knowing it when we adopt the patronizing attitude of, "I think it'll work out all right if you just take my advice." The important thing is to get the problem solved, not to get credit for solving it. The thing that may make the solution most effective is our ability to convince the employee that it was his or her solution.

Finally, if possible, keep employees' problems confidential. Avoid putting those problems into their personnel records, especially when they have come to you expecting to get private counsel. If there was a discussion about performance, or if the meeting resulted from a performance problem, then it may be necessary to put this in the files; but if appraisal records are open to others, we should be careful about putting anything about this meeting in those records unless employees are agreeable to it.

THE DISCIPLINARY INTERVIEW

Disciplinary interviews are difficult because they are different in purpose and origin from other types of interviews, and because they have the potential for being unpleasant. They are one of those undelegable necessities that supervisors have as a part of their job. The disciplinary interview is a basic requirement of our job and usually is not as bad as we expect it to be. The reason we have to have disciplinary interviews is that employees sometimes fail to meet performance requirements or they break rules. We have to have rules, regulations, and standards of the job, but not everyone meets every standard all the time. When employees fail to meet the standard too often or by too great a margin, we have to discipline them—or change the standard. We simply can't run a company or organization in which people continually fail to meet the standards set by those in position to know what a good standard is. Nothing lowers morale more quickly or destroys our effectiveness as a supervisor more completely than allowing someone to break the organization's rules constantly. For example, if we set a precedent by letting one rater get away with sloppy, incomplete work, we have little chance of stopping others who decide to try the same thing. It's equally hard on the conscientious employee who wants to abide by the rules if some employees are allowed to do otherwise. Even if only one employee habitually comes in late, there should be no exceptions to the hours that have been established and accepted.

A positive attitude is the best one to take toward a disciplinary interview. For the good of all concerned something needs to be done. If the problem is allowed to continue, nothing but trouble can result. The unit or department is suffering because of the situation, and it doesn't make good sense to let things get worse because we dread doing something unpleasant. Not only is our organization not functioning at its best but also our job is harder because of the problem; and we, too, are failing to operate as well as we can. We are probably having to cover up, redo, make excuses, or explain to others because of the situation that one employee has gotten us into, so we have every right to attack the problem head-on. We have already seen that the others in the group are going to become involved, especially if the situation is allowed to continue without corrective action, so for the good of the others in the work group we need to do something in a hurry. Even the employees who cause the problems suffer from them, because their careers are in jeopardy. Regardless of how unpleasant the interview may appear, the reasons for conducting it are real enough. If we do a good job and get the problem solved, we will be the stronger for it; and all concerned will be happier and better employees as a result. Two things are worthy of note here: No matter how much we dread the interview, it won't get any easier if we put it off; and this kind of interview is usually not as bad as we expect it to be.

The process

Disciplinary interviews begin just like the others. Our first action is to put our interviewees at ease, going through the steps we have discussed.

The worst thing we can do is to confront the employee angrily the minute he or she walks into the office. If we feel that our temper is going
to explode, then we'd better postpone the interview until we calm
down. We must remind ourselves that all our employees are valuable
and that we mustn't do anything to cause them to become less valuable.
We aren't trying to win a battle, we're trying to get the organization
back to running the way it should be. We aren't trying to prove any
points, neither are we trying to prove that any interviewee is wrong and
we are right. We are simply trying to correct a situation that cannot be
allowed to continue. Our employees must recognize from the moment
we begin talking to them that we are trying to be fair. Being fair means
that we want to hear their side of the matter and to know any facts
they might have to add to the total knowledge we have. This brings up
an important point. We must have adequate information before we start
the interview. Perhaps more than any other kind of interview, the disciplinary interview requires that we be fully informed. This is no time to
discover that we have our facts wrong or that we don't have the whole
story. And it's just as important to remember to have the facts substan-
tiated. When we say, "You've been late nearly every day this month,"
we aren't making a hard, factual statement. We'd do much better with
exact information, and say, "You've been late 14 days this month."
The difference between the two statements is the difference between
having or lacking confidence.

We must also be sure that employees know they're being disciplined. Sometimes we try to sandwich the disciplinary comments in
with praise, and the interviewees lose the message. If we wait until
they're about to leave and then say, "By the way . . .", and go into the
reasons for our calling them into the session, we've done both them and
ourselves an injustice. They should know from the start what the purpose of the interview is. They should know that their performance or
behavior has been unacceptable, and we should tell them what the
standard is and where they have failed to meet it. Just as clearly, we
should let them know what corrections are expected and when they
should take place. Of course, this isn't just a "tell, tell, tell" interview.
After we have stated the reason for the interview as quickly as possible
we should start to "listen, listen, listen." We want to be sure the interviewees have a chance to state their side of the question. There is always the possibility that there are some factors in their favor which we
haven't considered. If someone says, "My former supervisor told me it
was all right to underwrite trucking risks this way," or, "The customer
services department started doing this two months ago," we'd better be

prepared to study the matter further. At least if these things are so, we should know it.

Finally, we should deal with the employees' specific problems, not their total performance unless that total performance is in question. There's little to be gained by making interviewees look worse than they really are just to prove a point. We need to be ready to admit their strengths and be willing to praise them as the occasion arises. But we can't let the good points overshadow the bad, nor can we hide the fact that they are being called to answer for their conduct. Like most interviews, the disciplinary one needs to terminate with the same preciseness with which it begins. The longer we drag it out the more danger there is that we will begin to cloud the issue. Simply put, we need to deal with the problem, state the standard, state the acceptable or corrective behavior we expect from the employee, listen to all the facts, answer pertinent questions, be sure that he or she understands what happens now, and then end the interview. If possible, we end on a positive note of our expectations for better performance; we end on a pleasant note to show we expect things to work out; but above all, we end it.

THE EXIT INTERVIEW

As new supervisors, very few of us are likely to get the opportunity to conduct exit interviews, which are simply interviews with employees who have indicated in a positive way that they have decided to leave the company or organization. The purpose of these interviews isn't to try to persuade the employees to change their minds. Often supervisors do this and end up making things worse than they were when the employees decided to leave. Why then should we have interviews with people who are leaving, especially if we aren't aiming primarily at talking them into staying with the organization?

The reasons are obvious when we start to think about all the things we can learn from such interviews. As supervisors we occasionally need to check our perception. How well do we know the individuals who are leaving? Do we really know why they're leaving? Do we really know much about their relationship with their peers and the rest of the organization? Getting the answers to these questions out of the interviews will check our perception. Another reason for exit interviews is to monitor our abilities as supervisors. Do we have some weaknesses that could be corrected? Are we somehow at fault for the individual's leaving? Have we created a situation in the work group that may cause others to leave, too? These answers might also come out of the interview.

Another reason for the interview is to check the organization's policies and working conditions. Are we matching the wrong people with the jobs? Are we putting college grads into unchallenging jobs? Are our hiring procedures creating bad situations? Are our policies out of date or out of line with those of other organizations in the industry or in the community? Is there something wrong with our salary administration? The answers to all these questions may not be found in one interview, but clues may be seen in the things that are found out. So this is another reason for conducting exit interviews.

A final reason for these interviews is that they benefit the employees who are leaving. They may need to get some things off their chest. They may feel some remorse about leaving and the interview can help as they talk about the decision they have made. Most important, they may be heading into some future trouble that can be prevented by a calm and rational talk. All of these become logical, sound and compelling reasons for having the interview. But none of the results will be satisfactory if we do a poor job of conducting the interviews.

How do we conduct exit interviews? Superficially, this type looks similar to the others, but there are some important differences. As usual, we want to put the interviewees at ease and let them know that we appreciate their taking the time to talk to us, even though they've made up their mind to leave our company or agency. We must let them know quickly that we feel they can help us and that we'd appreciate their help. And we want to assure them that we are not going to try to change anyone's mind about leaving and that our every intention is to listen. We are looking for insight into our own problems and ways that we can improve the organization. Above all, we should put the interviewees at ease by letting them know we aren't going to pry or ask them to tell us irrelevant things about others in the group.

When an exit interview begins, we start listening. We ask open-ended questions designed to get the interviewees talking and keep them talking. We avoid interrupting them and do our best not to go on the defensive. We correct any statements about policy that are obviously untrue, but we don't have to defend them. No matter how much we'd like to describe the good results that these policies have, this isn't a time for us to emphasize that unduly. We want to keep disagreement to a minimum, so even when we correct a statement to supply the facts we do it by saying, "Well, it may have appeared that way, but actually the promotion-from-within policy reads . . . ." And when we come to a situation where there is no way to avoid disagreement, we need to say, "It's interesting that you feel that way," not, "You're crazy if that's the way you think."

Exit interviews have one unique hazard that must be anticipated and avoided. We must not let them degenerate into name-calling exchanges about people in the group. Unless there is a substantial amount of relevant evidence, there is no need to get into a discussion of specific employees. Even in the face of this evidence, there is no reason to talk about people unless there's something useful to be gained by it. If there's someone in the office or some policy or procedure in the organization that is a well known problem, this interview probably isn't the place to discuss it. It makes more sense to concentrate on those things that we can do something about. If interviewees want to talk about something that bothered them while they were working, even though it is something that shouldn't objectively have affected them, this, too, has no real priority in the discussion.

Use the information

In one respect exit interviews are like all other interviews we have—we must learn to use the information we get. It's useless to take the time to gather information if we don't use it after we get it. Exit interviews may be the most important of all from this standpoint. An intelligent use of the information from them may be the means of preventing or reducing exit interviews in the future! We should study the information and decide what we've learned and how we can use it. If we have found a bad situation, we should correct it if it is within our authority. If the information tells us that something we did caused a problem, we take the necessary steps to see that it doesn't happen again. Finally, we should review our own actions during these interviews to see if we are satisfied with the way we conducted them. We ask ourselves:

"Did I plan it well?"

"Did I put the employee at ease?"

"Did it go as I planned it?"

"Did I really accomplish anything?"

"How did the employee feel when it was over?"

"How did I feel when it was over?"

"If I had it to do over again, would I do it differently?"

If the answer to this last question is "Yes," then we need to take whatever steps are necessary to see that we actually do it differently the next time!

CONCLUSION

Successful interviews don't just happen; they are carefully planned. It is an oversimplification to say that an interview is simply two people talking to each other, but really that is just what it is. The purposes or objectives may differ from one interview to the next, the roles played by the interviewee and interviewer may change from one interview to the next, but the success of an interview comes down to our ability to talk with people. There are times when we're primarily seeking information, as in an employment interview. Sometimes we also want to give information, as in an appraisal interview. It may be that in a counseling interview we principally need to listen attentively and with empathy. But whatever kind we're involved in, we still are using the skills of talking with people on a one-to-one basis. We need to learn to plan the interview so we'll have a good idea of where we're going and when we've gotten there. To keep the person talking we have to learn to ask questions properly, perhaps open-endedly or by using a reflective technique. We might have to be direct and let the person know where he or she is missing the mark and what the consequences are for not making the correction. These things aren't always easy to accomplish, and to be really good at them we have to practice, study our results, and practice some more. We have to be practicing the right thing, though, because practice makes only permanent, not necessarily perfect. If we practice the wrong thing long enough, it will begin to feel natural to us.

Listening is by far the hardest part of learning how to communicate, but in an interview listening is most often the key to success. We can direct the interview by responding to whatever part of the interviewee's remarks we think will lead in the right direction, but this works only if we have been listening carefully to what is being said. Bad interviews result when we fail to take our turn at listening. This is more than just being quiet while the other person is talking, it's a matter of listening carefully, understanding, and responding properly. The steps in successful interviewing are simple enough to learn but take some concentration, mostly on setting our goals and then listening to see if we're getting the feedback that tells us we're going where we want to go. Once we've learned to be a good interviewer, it's surprising how much satisfaction we can get from conducting a successful interview. Since we're involved in so many interviews during our years as a supervisor, we must try for as much satisfaction as we can get.

EXERCISES

1. Group multiple role play: Have the group divide into subgroups of three each. One is to be the interviewer, one the interviewee,

and the other the observer. Those being interviewed are to play themselves. The idea is to find out each interviewee's viewpoint toward a promotion within the organization. The observer should look for the steps in successful interviewing, such as: putting the employee at ease; stating the purpose of the interview; asking open and reflective questions; dealing with questions; summarizing action to be taken as a result of the interview; and concluding the interview on good terms.

2. Group multiple role play: When the above role plays are completed, have the participants rotate positions, with the observer now being interviewed and the interviewee becoming the interviewer. The former interviewer becomes the observer. When this is over, have the people report their successes and failures. Record the things that were difficult to do, and areas where they need to improve.

3. Subgroup exercise: In small groups discuss why disciplinary interviews are feared and what we might do to overcome this feeling. Determine whether there is a justification for this and see whether anyone has had a bad experience with an employee they've had to discipline. Bring the large group back together and see what they've found out. Make a list of the most often used excuses for not doing disciplinary interviews.

4. Individual exercise: Ask the participants to think back about themselves as they were when they started with their present organization. Try to recall what questions were asked and list them down the left side of a piece of paper. On the right side of the sheet put a checkmark by those things that were really important to the job the person actually had. When all have finished, collect the typical questions and record on the board. Save for further use.

5. Group activity: Look at the items from Exercise 4 and decide what questions we really need to ask a person we're considering hiring. See if there are any questions that get into the interview through custom or tradition. See if we can eliminate any of them because they don't relate to the job to be done. This shouldn't be taken as an excuse for not asking anything! We do need much information, and the time to get it is before the employee comes to work with us.

10

TRAINING:
THE SUPERVISOR'S
RESPONSIBILITY

One of the biggest mistakes made by supervisors new and old is assuming that training is only an adjunct to their regular job—something they do only when they have plenty of time and nothing else to do. A supervisor who has this attitude really doesn't understand the essence of his or her job very well, since the distinctive function of the supervisor is to get work done through other people. Taking this another step, we can say that our prime job is to see that our clerical or technical staff is trained. If we have an employee who can't do his or her job because of a lack of training, then *we* have fallen down on the job as far as that person is concerned. Unless our people are properly trained, we have no real basis for appraising them or for finding fault with their performance. Training, then, is an important part of our job, and we must learn how to train others if we expect to succeed as supervisors.

TRAINING IS A SKILL

Unfortunately, many people still want to classify the ability to train others as either an art or a science. Maybe it is, but first and foremost it is a skill; and like any other skill it must be learned. Sometimes we tend to think of training others merely as something we can do without any special skill, thinking there's nothing hard about telling someone how to do something we know all about. The problem is that's often as far as we go, and we mistakenly think of training as "telling" someone how to do it. But telling isn't training.

There are many skills that we as supervisors have to learn. We must learn to write, speak, conduct interviews, and train our people. Unfortunately, we can do these things in such a way that to the casual observer it will look like we're doing all right when actually we aren't. We watch others doing training and it looks and sounds like they're doing a good job, but we may be fooled by what we see and hear. The employees being trained may not really get the message and may go away frustrated. The people doing the training may think they have done well and go about their business complacently thinking the employees should do their jobs satisfactorily. Later we may hear the trainers say to the technical or clerical staffer, "Don't you remember. I told you last week how to rate that policy?" The point is that employees often get the blame for the poor job of training done by the supervisors; so we must learn the skill of training others.

There are some supervisory skills we may put off learning, but we must become proficient trainers quickly if we are to get good performance from our people. Not only must we learn how to train others quickly, but we must also learn how to do it well. Every time we do a poor job of training our people, we waste time that can't be recovered; and we can fall into the painful dilemma of not knowing whether to train over again or let the employee go on doing the job only half well. Often the truth is that we rarely repeat the training, but we end up spending a lot of time trying to set right the poor results achieved by poorly trained employees. Of course, the worst finale that can occur is when we end up blaming our mail clerks, policy typists, or coders for not being able to do their jobs when really we've failed at ours.

We can learn the basic skill of training others if we recognize it as a skill and work hard at learning it. We cannot assume that just because we know the specific skill or task in which we're training the employees, we also know how to train someone on that job. Computing an insurance premium is quite different from training someone how to do it.

There are steps to training that we can identify and measure. We can improve on the skill once we learn what it is that makes up the skill, and we can tell whether or not we have done a good job. Let's take a look at the skill in more detail and see just what it is that makes up this thing that some want to take for granted.

WHY TRAIN?

If we ask whether training is necessary, the obvious answer is, "Of course." But if we ask why we train, we get some strange answers. Some organizations might train because there is money in the budget; others train because the employees expect it. There are those who train because higher management has directed that it be done. Others train only to fill up their spare time. None of these are valid reasons for training. Basically, there are only three good reasons for training:

1. The employee can't do the job (Example: can't code a health insurance policy; can't identify whether an insured has coverage or not).
2. The employee can do it but not well enough (Example: has an unacceptably high ratio of mistakes in rating auto insurance policies).
3. The employee is doing the job incorrectly (Example: is confusing the named insured with the beneficiary).

In the case of not being able to do the job, it may be that the employees are new and have never done it before. This is an obvious case for training, but there are those who say, "Experience is the best teacher. Let them learn to rate policies the hard way like I did." This isn't a practical approach from the standpoint of efficiency. Maybe the claim adjuster will be better able to do the job after he or she has made numerous mistakes, but in the meantime who pays for all those mistakes? Who helps the employees "unlearn" all the things they've learned to do incorrectly? If the employees are new, then for the benefit of both them and the organization, it's our job to see that they have an opportunity to start off learning the right way to do their jobs. Only then can we get an accurate picture of how well they're performing and progressing. But it may be that the job is a task that has never been performed before by anyone in the organization—say, handling a billing process via automation. It may be a new procedure, or a new piece of equipment, such as a computerized word processing system. Here, again, the employees have a right to get started on the right foot. Also, for the good of the new policy, procedure, or system, let's get the job done correctly from the beginning. Anytime we introduce something new there will be enough problems without our complicating things by doing a poor job of training.

The case of training because the employees can't do the job well enough isn't quite as simple as the first case. It may be that the employees haven't been trained and have picked up some of the job on their own. We need to speed up their production and save on wasted time; but now we are faced with the question of whether or not to train because the employees already know something about the job. We have to weigh or "trade-off" the time and expense of training against the advantages of doing the job faster or better. The same is true even if the employees actually had some training at one time but need more in order to meet the standards set for our organization. We have to decide what the cost benefit is to realize the improvement we can get from training.

Finally, there are the employees who are actually doing the job incorrectly. This is likewise valid ground for training. How do we know the policy typists aren't able to do the job? We may be able to tell just by the number of errors that can be traced directly to them; or it may be that an informal survey has caused us to look more closely at each typist and we see that some are failing to do their jobs correctly. It may also be that observing how the employees do their work convinces us quickly that they actually don't know what they're doing. This sounds like sufficient reason for training, but we need to ask ourselves one basic question before we do any training: "If the employees' lives depended on it, could they type the policies correctly?" If the answer to this is "yes", then training isn't the answer; there is some other supervisory problem involved and training won't solve it. So when we train, we must ask ourselves whether we are training to enable the employees to do the job, to enable them to do it better, or to enable them to do it correctly. We need to ask this question for each employee we train.

This appears simpler than it really is. If we aren't careful, we'll find ourselves training an employee who has had the training some time ago. To compound the challenge the employee's performance may even improve for some time right after the training, especially if he or she enjoys the change of pace from working at the job. But the chances are good that the employee will do fair-to-poor in the training session and go back to the job confused and wondering why we repeated the training. Even worse, we could end up giving training a bad reputation because the employee can't do the job any better after the training; some could generalize that training is a waste of time.

Another possibility for error is training someone who isn't going to have adequate time to apply what he or she learns. Maybe the employee is a senior property underwriter just a few months away from retiring or moving to a supervisory job. Everyone else in your unit or department has had the training, so we schedule this person for it, also. It's fine to consider our employee's feelings; but if we train this experienced employee because we don't want to hurt anyone's feelings, we need to remember that it's also good to worry about the company's money. How can we justify spending training money when it's obvious we can't get our investment back from an employee who just won't be on the job that long, whether the cause be impending retirement, promotion to a different job, or whatever?

There is yet another time when it is a mistake to train. When we train an employee we want to see promoted, we don't train because he or she needs it or can do a better job for us but because this particular training program might "look good" on his or her record. Unless this is a required part of the employee's regular development program, we've made a mistake in training for this reason. The problem may come back to haunt us. It may get around that we have set a precedent that anyone who takes this kind of training can expect to be promoted, or everyone may want to be sent to the training program because they think it's the way to move up. In either case, we've put an unfair burden on the training program and have asked it to do something it wasn't intended to do.

Finally, one other misuse of training that can get us into trouble is training someone we know doesn't have a chance to learn the job because of his or her background or lack of experience. Some supervisors send certain people to training programs to prove that the employee is incompetent; but if we do we've used training in the wrong way and have failed to do our job properly. The basic rule is to train the right people for the right reasons.

PREPARING TO TRAIN

Before we can do any effective training of our own, we must first determine just what it is we want to train our employees to do. This sounds simple enough, but it really isn't. For example, we should be sure we know exactly what standards of performance we are looking for. This means analyzing the job to make sure we can train someone else to perform according to the organization's standard—that is, to do the right thing in the right time with no more than the acceptable number of errors. The standard shouldn't always be what a gifted employee has done on that same job. Neither is it automatically what has come to be accepted as the average for employees doing this particular job. It's really what the organization has set as a standard for the job itself. We need to learn to set job standards by first analyzing the work, not the employees who are now or have been doing the job.

Before we train we should get policy questions settled. For example we'd better find out if there are procedural or equipment changes in the offing that will make our standards incorrect or irrelevant. If there are acceptable deviations from the job standard, we'd better know about them before we start to train. There's no reason to fear asking questions about standards, because we can never be sure later that our training has really been done properly if we don't know what the underlying standard actually is. Remember, many so-called standards exist because everyone has thoughtlessly accepted them without question, maybe even perpetuating error or mediocrity in the process. This is particularly true with things like work-flow. Just because filing cabinets were placed in a certain place at one time, we keep them there even though work may flow unevenly around them and it would be much more efficient to move them closer to the work operation. As a result of this poor arrangement, the work has suffered, but the historical "standard" has been set. If we don't watch out, we'll find ourselves training to this inferior standard.

We find this to be true also with such things as documents and forms. We try to train a clerk to fill out a complicated form or slip without ever asking the $64 question: Just why must this form be so complex? The truth may be that it evolved that way because periodically someone added something to it without ever trying to shorten or simplify it. Soon it got unwieldy, but we keep using it as the standard and try to train people to use it. A few thoughtful questions might help "uncomplicate" the form. In fact, just listening to our employees might help. They probably know that some things about it are unnecessary, but no one has bothered to ask them. Remember, they are the ones doing the job, so they are the most apt to be familiar with what is actually being done. If we can't develop a better reason for doing or not doing something a certain way, we should probably listen carefully to their ideas and views.

It's highly unlikely that we can ever train on everything in our department that needs attention, so we have to decide early just what it is we are going to include in the training program for each of the employees. For example, for new employees, we should concentrate on those things that will be likely to come up first in their new assignments. They'll have enough to do to learn the things they'll be doing immediately without needlessly diverting their attention to things that won't come up for months. If the job is being changed somewhat, we should concentrate on the changes, not spend time reteaching the entire job. It's wasteful and boring to the employees to repeat training in knowledge or skills that they already possess. Even after we decide what to do our training on, we should still check to see if there are any programs which already exist that will do the job for us. Maybe the company or organization already has some kind of program which will come close enough to doing our job for us that it isn't worthwhile for us to develop an entire training program "from scratch." By the way, we mustn't forget to check with other departments about their training programs. Sometimes we get so out of touch with others in the same organization that we forget they face the same training problems that we do and may be conducting programs very similar to the ones we are preparing. We should ask ourselves, "Who else might have the same kind of training problems I do?" The answer to this question should help us screen the market well enough to prevent us from inventing the wheel all over again.

Once we've decided on what training needs to be done and why we're doing it, we must set some realistic objectives or goals for the training we are going to do. The simplest way to do this is to ask, "What is it I want them to be able to do when the training is over?" Basically, the answer to this question depends on the answers to the following ones:

What actions do I want from them?

What standards do I plan to use to gauge their success?

What limitations or tolerances can I live with?

As we suggested earlier if we've taken a good analytical look at the job, these things should be clear. We should know what a satisfactory job is; and if we don't, it will show up when we attempt to answer these questions. It's not enough to just say, "We want them to understand how the typewriter works." We have to specify the action and the degree of tolerance we expect to allow. Requiring that the policy typist produce "X" items an hour or day with no more than a 2 percent error rate is much more specific than requiring that he or she understand how to use the machine. One reason training is sometimes not precise is that we are apt to think about it in a haphazard manner. We suddenly discover ourselves doing some training without much real planning; and when we do an inadequate job of planning, we will probably do inadequate training. The planning need not be elaborate or time-consuming; it may even be written out on the back of an envelope, but it should be done. We need to decide where the training is going to take place, who will be trained, and when it will be done.

DO IT RIGHT

It seems redundant to say it, but when we train, we should do a good job of it. As obvious as that sounds, we still find that some people do a much better job of training than others. The reasons for this is that we don't always know good training when we see it. Supervisors can be heard to say, "Don't you remember, I told you that the rate for that territory was on page 10". Again, this means that they think "telling" and "training" are the same. In fact, when we watch them "train," they invariably do most of the talking and the showing, then end with a statement like, "Any questions?" The employees think they understand. The operation looked simple enough; but after the supervisor leaves, the employees find that they can't really do the job after all. They feel pretty stupid because they've just seen the supervisor do it and heard an explanation about which they didn't have any questions—all because the supervisor did a poor job of training. Since training is a skill, we can't expect to be good at it right away. But we can learn the skill; and as we do we can evaluate the results and grow in the skill.

Good training follows specific steps and procedures. When we train people on the job, what we do will have a definite bearing on how well they can perform in the future. The most accepted way is to use is a simple, three-step process that has worked well for many years. It goes like this:

STEP 1

We tell them what to do. ("Enter the premium due in the correct block.")

We do it correctly.

STEP 2

They tell us what to do. ("Next, determine what page the agent's account is on.")

We do it correctly.

STEP 3

They tell us what to do. ("Indicate whether the prospect has installed a burglar alarm.")

They do it correctly.

Note the purpose of each step. In Step 1, we tell the employees what is to be done so there will be no doubt about the action and so they will be mentally involved. Then we do it correctly, being sure they see each part of the procedure. In Step 2, they are still mentally involved as they tell us what to do; and if they tell us correctly, we do it correctly again. In Step 3, they tell us what they're going to do but don't do it until we have agreed that they're right. If they are, then we let them do it. Step 3 can be repeated several times for practice, but it's always a good idea to keep the employees involved mentally as much as possible because this is where memory is established. Even though we want the employees to develop good work habits, we still want them to perform from a positive mental attitude. To increase this mental involvement, we can expand the three-step process to include not only "what", but also "why" and "how". We still go through each step as described above; but after going through "what", we repeat the process by telling "how". Then we repeat, telling them why we perform the operation the way we are doing it. In other words, the first time through we concentrate on the employees' seeing, hearing and doing the right thing. They see how, but at this point we don't treat it in much detail. Then we repeat the process, this time adding a description of how we do it so that the employees hear a description of the correct way to perform the operation while they're doing it. Finally, we go over the "what" and "how" and add to it the reasons why we do it a certain way.

It should be obvious that when we are doing this kind of training, we have the employees use the actual equipment or something that looks just like what they will be using. Ideally, they should be trained on the equipment they use every day right at the spot where they will actually do the job. If not, then we should try to find idle equipment that is like the kind they'll be using. As a final alternative, we can use something that closely simulates the regular equipment they will use; but we should remember that the less they have to use their imagination, the better they will be trained. For example, if they consult rating manuals on the job, they should have rating manuals in training. If they write on blue paper on the job, they should have blue paper during the training. By the way, there's a key point here that is easy to overlook. When we train, we never face the employees; we always show them from the same position they will take when they do the work. If we face them, they will see everything done backwards and may become quite confused when they try doing it themselves.

CLASSROOM TRAINING

Occasionally supervisors will be asked to conduct some form of classroom training. It may be that they have become expert in certain fields, such as liability underwriting or fire insurance rating, or have been selected to study a particular subject and teach in an organizational school of some kind. Occasionally supervisors have enough employees working for them that they find it easier to do the training all at one time in some kind of classroom setting. For that reason we'll describe briefly how to do this kind of training effectively. First, there is more to teaching a group than merely having a knowledge of the subject, and there is more to it than being able to make a good speech. The ultimate objective is the same as in on-the-job training—to change some people's behavior on the job. Up to this point, everything we've said about preparing for on-the-job training applies also to classroom training. We have to know what it is we want the people to be able to do. There needs to be a performance standard of some type, and it helps if we know the strengths and deficiencies of the people in the class. Once we've done this and found out what we need to know about the standards and the performance strengths and needs of the employees, we're ready to go into the classroom. Let's see what we need to know to make this effort effective.

There are some basic rules for classroom training that will help us understand our job better. First, people learn more by participating in the learning activity than they do by being told what they need to know. We can tell them much faster if they aren't involved in saying or doing things, but they can forget just as fast! Next, we should realize that the students are more likely to remember those things they figure out for themslves than those we figure out for them. This means that we need to let them "discover" some of the information for themselves, especially the conclusions. In some circles this technique is called discovery learning, and that's a good name for it because that's exactly what happens. The instructor gives the class members enough information to enable them to figure out the rest on their own; the instructor leads them along with new information, building on what they already know, then stops with a question aimed at making them think about where all of this is leading. At this point, if we've done the job right, they'll get a big "Aha!" reaction; and we'll have caused them to discover what it was we wanted them to learn. As a result they'll remember it longer.

The next thing to keep in mind is that they will be more likely to remember and learn those things that relate most to their jobs. If they are given some information or shown some kind of new operation with the knowledge that they will be expected to use it when they get back on the job, they'll be much more likely to work at learning it than if they hear, "Some day you may need to know these territorial rate differences, so you'd better pay attention." The good instructor will build in examples of application of these things, and have good illustrations of incidents in which the employees can use the new knowledge or skill back on the job. Obviously, not all employees or students have the same background, the same interest in learning or the same ability to grasp all the subjects. This brings up another thing to remember: If they aren't all learning the same way, we may have to teach in different ways to reach different ones. For some a lecture may be fine because in high school or college they learned to grasp quickly from a lecture. For others repeating may be important, because it takes a while for them to grasp the material. Still others may require some discussion, different examples, or different approaches. All of these approaches might have to be combined in each teaching session because we can't always tell immediately which students are learning best in which way.

This leads us to the next point in making ourselves good instructors.We'll know what's being learned by whom *only* when we hear them tell us or see them showing us. In teaching jargon, this is called "getting feedback." We talked about the importance of it in our discussion of communications (Chapter 5), and for the same reasons it's extremely important in our teaching efforts. If we pay attention only to what we're saying, we won't know what the students are learning. If we get feedback from only one or two, we'll have a general idea of how well we're doing; but we won't know for sure how the entire class is doing until we hear *all* of them saying things and reacting to what we've been teaching. When we mention feedback, the idea of testing comes to mind; but this isn't what we're talking about here. For example, by having the class break into small groups and come up with an agreement on an assigned discussion question, we can find out in matter of a few minutes how well we've gotten our point across. If there is much discussion and little agreement, we'd better start over or review. If they come up with a common answer quickly, we can reinforce this and go on.

While we're talking about differences in the classroom, we should point out that one very good way of overcoming the problem of differences is to have the less experienced class members work with the more experienced ones, the less interested with the more interested, or the slower learners with the quicker. This puts some of the responssibility on the better students, and they will actually learn more as they try to help others along. Much of the time, students learn from one of their classmates as well as, or better than, they do from the instructor.

We said that good teaching is more than good public speaking. Let's emphasize that bad public speaking—that is, mumbling, distracting mannerisms, poor use of the visual aids equipment, etc.—has to be overcome by even better teaching techniques. We can ruin some good instructional efforts by poor speaking efforts. Our students won't necessarily get more from the speaking itself if it's polished and "stage-worthy," but at least we won't detract from the learning effort if we make a good try at speaking well!

FOLLOW UP ON TRAINING

One final word about training: We shouldn't just train and go off and leave it. We should follow up on what we have done and see how well the training "took." Training is more than doing it, marking the training record, then forgetting about it and the employees, saying, "Well, that job is complete." We should go back to the employees on the job and see how they're doing. We should check their performance against the performance standard we set, check error rates, look at output, see if the job is complete, or check on how they're doing whatever we trained them to do. If the employees are performing well, we can take credit for a job well done. If not, then we need to take a look at our procedures to see if *we* failed to do the job properly. The rule in this case is simple. If the employees are doing something we trained them on, we are responsible for their performance until we determine that something other than their training is keeping them from doing the job. Of course, we are always responsible for their performance in a way, but now we look for some other cause because we are satisfied that the training has been done correctly. If we follow the proper procedures, we can be sure that the training has been done correctly.

CONCLUSION

Training is the supervisor's responsibility. That's the heading of this chapter and it's the message within it. It's the conclusion we need to accept when we study training. Training subordinates to reach their potential is our job and there can be serious consequences if we don't do it correctly. The ironic thing about poor training is that often it isn't the supervisor but the poorly trained employees themselves who get the blame. Although their records show that they were trained, their job performance is suffering; and they will be shown as below-standard performers on those records. To make it worse, the employees may think they've been trained and give themselves a bad self-image, perhaps believing they just aren't capable of learning. To emphasize the need to do a good job of training, let's think of it in this way:

It's now performance appraisal time, and technical and clerical employees are going to be evaluated on how well they've done in their jobs over a certain period of time. Hopefully there is a performance standard that is understood by both them and us and that tells how well they should be doing those jobs. However, if we've failed to train them properly, they can't perform up to that standard, and we really have no right to appraise them. Suppose we've done a so-so job of training them and the training is entered on their official records. But because they have not had effective training, they obviously are not doing their jobs up to standard. In the appraisal interview we simply note on an employee's record that he or she isn't performing the job up to standard and let it go at that. To be honest and fair shouldn't we really write, "Due to poor training, this employee has not yet been able to perform up to standard?" Of course, we aren't likely to make such an entry, but in the future the employee could suffer from the negative appraisal.

Now think about the whole situation from the standpoint of having done a good job of training. It's now appraisal time, and our employees are doing their jobs up to standard. Even though we aren't likely to say that they are doing well because we did such a good job of training, we can take the satisfaction of knowing that when we did our job properly our employees responded with good performances which will be indicated on their records. We can be pleased with this kind of result, especially if we get it often. And we can get it often, if we learn our training skills well!

EXERCISES

1. Two-group exercise: Divide the group into two sections. Have one section take the position that training is a skill that has to be learned, can be measured, and can be done poorly or well or in between. Let them develop their arguments in favor of this in small subgroups within their section. One person should serve as their spokesperson. The other half of the group should operate the same way, in small subgroups and with a spokesperson for the entire half-group. Their position is that good training is an art that comes from being naturally gifted as an instructor. Some few things can be learned but for the most part a person either is or is not a good instructor, and trying to develop the skill will not aid appreciably. When the subgroups have finished their activity and combined their findings within their own sections, each section's spokesperson should be briefed for a discussion as outlined in Exercise 2 below.

2. Group exercise: the two sections should debate their sides now and should list their key points on the board or on a flip chart. All group members should be urged to take notes from each section's discussion. When the two sections have completed their discussion, the group as a whole should take a look at the points made and determine how valid they are. "Sides" should no longer be considered at this point; rather, everyone should begin to look at the points made with an eye to seeing how best to learn the skill of teaching.

3. Small-group activity: Divide the whole group into several small subgroups, each of which should pick a job or task that is common to all of its members, or at least familiar enough so that each member can contribute something in the discussion and exercise. The job should be a simple one or perhaps just a part of a job. Each subgroup should analyze the job they have selected, a step at a time, until they have it broken down. They should set a performance standard for each of the operations. The standard should tell not only how the job is to be done, but how well or how often in a period of time, etc. In other words, the standard should be measurable and observable. When the subgroups have gotten this information, they should be ready to present it to the entire group, having picked a spokesperson to represent them.

4. Group activity: Using the information on performance standards from Exercise 3, let each spokesperson present his or her findings, with the rest of the subgroup doing the "defending." The idea is for the whole group to see that we often try to train on things for which we haven't set a standard, hence shouldn't expect to do too good a job of training. (If we don't know how well we want the employees to perform, how can we know how well we've trained them?)

11
HOW TO RUN
A GOOD MEETING
(CONFERENCE LEADERSHIP)

Though very little of it is complimentary, much has been said about all of the meetings that are usually run in a company or organization. Committees meet, groups meet, managers meet, supervisors meet and meet some more. There is little chance that we will change this and we really don't want to. Meetings are a way of life and, to a large extent, the necessary thread of life in most organizations. The reason we sometimes make fun of them or complain about them is that they take up (and often seem to waste) a lot of our time—and they usually come at a time when we just don't have a moment to spare. It may just be, however, that one of the main reasons we feel as we do about meetings is that we've never experienced the satisfaction of attending and being part of a well-run meeting—one that accomplishes specific goals, does it quickly and efficiently, and terminates when the purpose has been met. It's to this end that this chapter is dedicated. We are going to try to establish the basis for conducting meetings that do just these things.

PREPARING FOR THE CONFERENCE

As we have said, conferences (meetings) are a way of life in the organization. Without proper control they can run poorly and accomplish very little. Run properly, they can bring about results that cannot be accomplished in any other way. The first fact we need to accept is that meetings have a precise purpose. They are necessary, hence we should approach them with a positive attitude and with some idea of what the particular purpose of any specific meeting is. Is it a problem-solving session? Have problems arisen that we need to attack in a group? If so, we must approach the meeting with the information needed for problem-solving; and we need to set it up so we can go through the steps in problem-solving. Is the purpose of the meeting decision-making? If so, we need to remember that no one should leave the meeting without knowing exactly what final decision was reached. We need to remember that someone must be responsible for carrying out that decision. In other words, we need to aim everything about the conference at decision-making. This requires good decision-making techniques in the meeting; and since we are leading the meeting, we are responsible for seeing that these techniques are followed.

Is the purpose of the meeting brainstorming? Has someone decided that the best way to reach a solution, develop an idea, or attack a problem is to have a group of people get together and do some brainstorming? If so, we must be sure that all the conditions of brainstorming are met and that we understand the process. We must have the necessary supplies for recording the ideas and have ourselves conditioned to avoid letting any negative thinking get into the session. Again, since we are conducting the meeting, it is our responsibility to see that everything goes well. But we must first establish the purpose in our minds so we can make the necessary arrangements.

Perhaps the purpose of the meeting is attitude development. For example, we may need to increase service consciousness to policyholders or improve advertising support for agents. Or maybe there is a computer-triggered quality-control problem and this meeting is for the purpose of changing attitudes toward this matter. If so, we need to know it, and to aim in that direction. Even if the meeting is just for the purpose of educating our group on new policies or services, we should settle this in our minds and build our planning around it.

The point is that if we are going to run the meeting, we need to know its specific purpose. We're asking a number of people to give up work time and come to the meeting, and they have a right to expect us to know what the real objective of the conference is and what we together will try to accomplish. As conference leaders, then, we ask ourselves, "What specific activities will take place?" This is important in the arrangement of furniture, the selection of equipment, the choice of rooms, etc. The activities will determine whether we will need to seat everyone in a circle, provide tables, or maybe just set up chairs facing the front in classroom style. Thinking of these things ahead of time will help make the meeting a success, but we need to know more. We should decide on the specific time for the meeting, not just how long it will run. When will we have it? What day? What time of day? If it's to be a one-hour meeting, why run it at a time that would conflict with an already established work schedule? If it's to be a lengthy one, we should provide for a break in the middle as a good way to inject some change of pace. A meeting at the end of the day or week, when everyone is tired and thinking about going home, might not be the best time to get into a brainstorming session. If we aren't sure how long the meeting will take, running it too close to lunch or quitting time may get us into trouble. Suppose it turns out that we need more time! What often happens here is that when time starts to run out and we don't want to have to call another meeting, we begin to make hurried decisions or leave some things hanging loose. When the meeting is over and we review our accomplishments, we discover that some important things got overlooked or that some of the things we decided aren't really very practical after all. Finally, on specifics, the conference leader needs to know the specific attendance—not just how many are going to attend, but who. There is always the consideration of seating, both who sits where and how many seats will be required. If the leader has any control over the selection of those who attend, he or she needs to go back and look at the meeting's specific objective. If this is to be an education or straight information-type meeting, then maybe the more people in attendance the better. On the other hand, if it is to be a problem-solving or decision-making session, the number needs to be held to some practical number. The basic requirement for the latter kind of meeting is enough people to represent all interests concerned, but not so many that it is weighted with people on one side of the question or from one department. Conferees don't like to be put in the position of having the meeting stacked against them in numbers. They have just as much right to their opinion as others, but if the "other side" brought along more than their share of representatives, then things are unequal. The conferees will know this in a hurry, too. The way to avoid this is to look at the list of suggested attendees and decide whether there is fair representation from all departments, groups, factions, etc. If not, a telephone call or private suggestion may be the best way to solve the problem. As we have said, these things make a lot of difference in the outcome of conferences, and conference leaders should do whatever they can to control the number and the mix of those attending.

PHYSICAL FACILITIES

Of all the things that can make or break a meeting, perhaps nothing can have more influence than the place where the meeting is held and the equipment used in the meeting. No matter how well the leader coordinates the timing, the speaking, the interchange of ideas, and the movement of information, all of this will accomplish very little if the room is poorly ventilated or is too hot or too cold. Actually, setting up the facilities isn't difficult when we consider some basic elements. We can divide the problem areas as follows:

Creature comforts

Acoustics

Visibility

Interference

Let's look at them individually beginning with the creature comforts—those things that affect our senses. Is the air being changed frequently enough by the ventilating system? Is there a means of regulating the temperature in a hurry if the room gets to hot or too cold? If at all possible, we want to be sure to have control of the temperature. If someone somewhere else can regulate the temperature in our room, we could have a problem and the same is true if the system is centrally controlled. If the only control we have is to open and close doors and windows, we might want to consider whatever alternative facilities are available. Many other things affect our comfort, some of which are subtle. For example, we can sit in a molded plastic chair that at first feels comfortable; but after a time it can become very uncomfortable because it was molded for one position and we don't sit in one position very long. As soon as we change from the position the chair was molded for, we're in a chair that doesn't fit us. Many people find it difficult to remain comfortable very long in chairs that don't have arms. As long as there is a table to lean on its not too bad, but when they try to lean back or relax, their arms drop to their sides in a strained way. This brings up another factor that's easy to overlook—the height of the table above the chair. If the table is too high or too low, the conferees find themselves straining to get comfortable. We need to remember that these aren't problems we can solve in a few moments. If we want to try out the furniture beforehand, we must try several positions—sitting with our arms on the table and then at our sides, leaning back in the chair, or sitting in one position for a few minutes. How does all of this feel? (How will it feel at the end of a three-day meeting?) Remember, too, that there is the possibility of being over-comfortable. If the meeting is likely to produce a few periods of boredom, soft easy chairs won't add to the alertness of the group.

The matter of acoustics is obviously important, and there are some problems that may not be apparent from just looking at a facility. For example, sound carries better in an empty room than in a full one. Even if the room appears to carry our voices very well, we still need to know if it will be all right when there are several people in the room. One way to check this is to have someone stand at one end of the room while we are at the other end and have them talk in a low, conversational tone, as if they were talking to someone next to them. Often that's how people talk in meetings. Even then we can't be positive, of course, because we can't regulate how low the participants will talk. The rule is to prepare for the minimal or "worst case" conditions, not the normal or average conditions.

Visibility is always a problem and can cause an otherwise good meeting to founder. If the meeting is to be built around charts, movies, or other visuals, then all those attending must be able to see or obviously they won't get much out of the meeting. But that's not the only challenge; even if the people are to be seated at a table and no visuals are to be used, they still like to see the speaker. This should be considered when the chairs are arranged and the tables are set out. Many meetings are ruined because all of the people are aligned along two sides of a table. Each time someone says something, everybody leans way over to try to see what is happening. Each has to lean out farther than the last, and pretty soon some are saying to themselves, "What's the use?"

Interference at a key point in the meeting can cause a setback, especially if we have spent valuable time building up our case. Just about the time we're making our final point and hoping for concurrence from the group, the maintenance man comes walking through with a ladder swinging over the heads of the people in the meeting. "Sorry folks, but this is the only way to get to the next room to check out that light bulb!" While we weep inside, the group starts trying to remember where they were a few minutes ago. Just as with acoustics, we can't check for interference just by standing in the middle of the room and listening one time. We should know about the room next door. We have to know what the hall sounds like when everyone on that floor takes a break and heads for the restaurant or cafeteria at the same time. Is there a kitchen next door where dishes will be rattling during lunch period? Do they use a high-powered vacuum cleaner on the rugs every Friday morning? These types of interference are obvious, and with a little planning and checking the person conducting the session can often avoid them. But there is another kind of interference that is much more subtle—the aide who brings the boss a message, calls the boss to the telephone, or tells the boss his or her plane tickets are ready. It's not really important why the assistant is there, but just the fact that someone comes in affects the meeting. While trying to be efficient, the aide may hurt the chances for a successful meeting. A "Do Not Disturb" note on the door can help, but arranging for someone to take and deliver messages at break periods is a much better guarantee. An extra sentence in the announcement of the meeting could solve the problem: "If you're expecting any messages during the meeting, have them left with Bill Jones, my assistant, at Ext. 7953."

CONDUCTING THE CONFERENCE

Our role as leader may vary from meeting to meeting and even during any particular meeting. This is why it is so important to know the exact purpose of the meeting. If we know this, we can more easily tell what our role is. Our primary function is to see that somebody takes all of the roles required to run a good meeting, which may mean that we will have to assume those not taken by others. If we are in charge of the meeting, the best approach we can take is to assign roles effectively to others. Put someone in the "initiating" role, someone else in the "timekeeping" role, yet another in the "support" role, etc. This way we can keep up with what is going on and know when to step in and take over a role not being taken by someone else; or we may need to reassign roles that are not being taken very well by others. The thing to remember is that effective leaders aren't necessarily seen and heard all of the time; they simply see that everything runs smoothly, regardless of who is seen and heard the most. Most often we mistake the word "leader" to mean the person who stands up, gives the direction, or moves the meeting on to the next point. We may do this, or we may assign the role to someone else because we know they have a lot of ability at that particular function.

HIDDEN AGENDAS

One frustrating thing about many meetings is that there often exist undercurrents of thoughts, needs, ideas, and objectives that never quite get out into the open. These have been correctly called hidden agendas and are simply those personal objectives that people bring to meetings that may differ from the real purpose of the meeting. Even though the stated purpose of the meeting may be to discuss overtime in a certain department, we may really want to say a few things about tardiness rules, and maybe get some possible answers on the subject. As decisions are being made, we may appear to be basing our suggestions on plain common sense or the needs of the group; but we may have a hidden agenda which tells us that certain things would be more popular with the boss or make our department look better. It is difficult to pinpoint every agenda that is brought to the meeting by each member of the group, but we should be aware that they are often there. We should also be aware that they will affect the meeting because they can produce biased answers. The first time we get an answer that surprises us because it doesn't sound reasonable or relevant in terms of the discussion so far, we may want to look to see if a hidden agenda is at work. We should ask ourselves, "What else could make Bob say that about our billing policy? Has he said something else before that indicates there might be pressure working on him back in the department? Is he trying to protect his job, his manager, or his collection staff?" The key is that we don't necessarily have to take any action to try to change the agenda Bob is apparently working with; we'll just be sure to weigh and consider what he says in terms of what we think his needs are. We must avoid trying to become a mind reader and realize that we may never know exactly why people react the way they do. In fact, they themselves may not even know; but if we see them beginning to fit a pattern, we should be sensitive to what they're doing and why. If we feel sure that we know what's causing them to react the way they are, we may even make this work for us. If we have reason to suspect that someone has a hidden agenda that will cause him or her to be budget conscious, we can include ideas about things being relatively inexpensive and even draw that person out on these items. On the other hand, we might try to avoid getting such a person involved in matters that deal with unusually large cost increases. (We don't hide or sidestep these matters, but neither do we overreact or make great issues out of them.

FEEDBACK

One signal that hidden agendas exist in our group is the kind of feedback we get from the participants. Without the proper amount of feedback we often can't tell how the group feels, what individuals are thinking, what direction we should take, or how well we are doing at directing the conference toward its goal. But though it's obvious why we need feedback, it isn't apparent how we get it. Let's look at some ways of getting it, remembering that the purpose is to use the infomation toward guiding the meeting and reaching the objectives we have set.

If the group is small, it shouldn't be too difficult to get the feedback. Usually a small group means less formality, hence everyone is saying what he or she thinks. At least it isn't hard to get the participants to answer a question directed to them, and they may even volunteer to give their opinions. As the size of the group increases, the problems of getting feedback increase, often on a geometric scale. Now we have to use some techniques that will more or less force the participants to give us the feedback we need. Actually this isn't so difficult, but it takes a little more effort. For example, we can simply go around the room and ask for comments on specific subjects. We can occasionally ask for a show of hands for both agreement and disagreement, but we need to be careful interpreting this. Even if no one raises a hand to show disagreement, it does not necessarily mean that everyone agrees. There are always those who won't hold up their hands but who still disagree. In this case we watch and see who doesn't hold up a hand for either yea or nay, then ask them how they feel. If nothing else productive happens, at least it will get them in the habit of responding one way or the other. Since people coming to the meeting are supposed to be representing certain viewpoints, they aren't doing their job properly if they don't express themselves. We shouldn't hesitate to help them along by asking direct questions, remembering that they are supposed to be there to help out. This doesn't mean that we try to embarrass them, but it does mean that we can ask them questions like, "We haven't heard from you, Jean. What do you think about changing the mailroom workflow?" Another technique we can use is to have the participants talk first in small groups on assigned subtopics and then report to the whole group. This way they iron out their differences in the small sessions and not before the entire group. Often they just want to be sure they have had a chance to be heard, and are just as satisfied to do it before a small group as before the whole meeting. The leader can see that good ideas get out before the entire group by listening to the small subgroups and then, when the larger group reforms, by giving one member or another a cue such as, "Didn't I hear you saying that Saturday overtime wasn't really a problem in your office anymore?" We do this when they fail to bring out the points we want brought out. We want to avoid suggesting that we already know what we want them to say and that if they don't say it, we'll do it for them. Nothing can kill their incentive any quicker.

What do we do with this feedback once we have gotten it? We use it to control and direct the meeting. We see where the participants are and how far along they are. If they aren't doing as well as we think they should be, we take steps to move along faster. If they are on schedule, we make note of it and keep on the same track. If they seem to be ahead of where we had thought they would be, we may even do some thinking about concluding the meeting early or planning on additional things we might undertake in the meeting. But that isn't the only function of the feedback. This is also a good way to get commitment. If we hear them say something that we want them to support when they leave, we can have them emphasize it in the meeting. "How about going over that again, Jim. I think that's the best analysis of our absentee problem I've heard so far." Another use for feedback is to give us a bridge or transition to move on to the next subject. When we have exhausted a subject and find it's time to go on, the ideal way is to do it by using some of the feedback: "O.K., Mona, that really takes us to the next subject, doesn't it? The way you have expressed it is. . . ." The transition is smooth and we don't appear to be completely dominating the session. Mona gets credit for initiating something new, the group gets an introduction to what is going to be talked about, and we know things are running smoothly.

CONFLICT

It would be unrealistic not to accept the fact that we can occasionally expect to run into some conflict in meetings. Our first inclination when we meet conflict is to think it's bad and may ruin our fine meeting. Of course, too much conflict can ruin a meeting, but a certain amount should be expected, and indeed planned for. We've already seen that people carry hidden agendas, so we shouldn't think that the meeting, in and of itself, has caused the conflict. Also, when people feel strongly enough about something to cause conflict among themselves and others, that means they are involved and have some commitment on the subject being discussed. We should be glad this is the case and try our best to use it to enhance the meeting. First we need to be sure to recognize conflict when it comes up in the meeting. Snide remarks, digs at other conferees, and other such obvious things aren't hard to recognize as symptoms of conflict. More subtle signs are withdrawals, over-politeness, too-quick committal, and frequent efforts to go back and discuss topics that have obviously been closed. There is no reason to let conflict degenerate into open hostility such as name-calling, shouting, etc. We keep this from happening by stepping in before it gets this far. But what should we do when we step in? Do we just say, "Now let's not have any conflict"? Hardly. The best thing to do is to use the situation to our advantage by formalizing the debate, thus relieving some of the steam, or by trying to state the conclusions of each side, thus directing the attention away from the disagreeing participants and back to us. By restating the positions and by adding more facts or data, we can often resolve the conflict. But we may not want to resolve it too quickly, for with it we have involvement, interest, and participation while without it we may not have any of these desirable conditions. When there is conflict, at least we know people are giving us their opinions. We see others taking sides, thus committing themselves. In a way we are getting some of the best, most spontaneous, candid feedback we could hope for. As long as it is productive, let's keep it going; when we feel it has done all the good it can do and may be starting to do some harm, we can step in and move on the next point. We do this in a number of ways, either by taking a stand ourselves and asking for commitment from all concerned or by gradually working our way into the conversation and turning it to more productive fields. Another way, which admittedly is not the best but is often necessary, is to point out in a straightforward way that though the situation is interesting, it probably isn't getting us very far. If conflict persists, we may have to postpone a portion of the meeting to a later date until the conflict can be resolved. Hopefully, the people engaged in the conflict will withdraw or give in some so that postponement won't be necessary. Most often the group as a whole will put enough pressure on the individuals to cause the situation to work itself out and thereby eliminate the need for another meeting.

MOTIVATING THE CONFEREES

Most people who are good at conducting meetings or conferences have learned a simple skill. They challenge the other conferees to help make the meeting a good one; they share the leadership roles. They recognize that it takes more than one person in a meeting to get the job done, so they don't just allow group members to assume various roles but plan to get them into those roles. For instance, they've learned that if somebody else does a naturally good job of summarizing, let him or her do it. If somebody is conscious of the time and reminds the group about deadlines, the leader thanks that person for remembering the time factor and doesn't resent it at all. If somebody plays the devil's advocate, asking questions and taking the opposite side to test the ideas being discussed, then let him or her do it because that role needs to be played and it's best played by one of the members. Good leaders know that when people participate in a meeting and think of it as their own, they'll be much more likely to support the results that come out of it.

To understand this best, we have only to remember the last meeting we went to where the leader played *all* the roles. The leader kept us on track; the leader reminded us of the time; the leader interrupted the long-winded participant; the leader praised good ideas and questioned bad ones. The leader asked, "Will people really support that idea?" The leader negotiated compromise among varying positions and thought; the leader introduced new ideas when things began to wind down too soon; the leader brought out those who weren't talking or contributing. When we watch such a person, we might think that he or she is doing a remarkably good job. We might even think of patterning ourselves after this leader, thinking how nice it was to have everything under control. But there is something wrong with this approach to conference leading. The problem is simple: It was never anybody's meeting but the leader's. Everyone let the leader have it, sat back and in essence said, "What do you want me to do now?" They contributed only when they were told to and stopped when told to. They were supporting the LEADER, not the reason for the meeting. It never was THEIR meeting, and the end product isn't theirs either. They probably won't be excited about how things go; and if things go wrong, they'll feel sorry for the leader, not for themselves and their effort.

Successful conferences are the result of thoughtful leaders sharing the meeting and the purpose with the conferees. The leaders begin the planning with this in mind and never lose sight of their objective. It's always "our meeting." It's always "we need to solve this problem." When people are invited, they are often told what they can contribute that others can't and are urged to do so. When they arrive, each is greeted as a special person bringing ideas and solutions and ability to tackle the problem at hand. If some have something special to report, their names are on the agenda and mention is made of it at the start to give them proper recognition. Roles—such as someone to take notes and someone to serve as timekeeper—may be assigned to people who are willing to play those roles. The good leaders will observe people falling into certain roles and let them do so. If someone seems good at sensing the need for a compromise and starts working toward that end, he or she is allowed to go ahead without interruption. A good leader will make a mental note of this and will call on this person later if it seems a compromise needs to be worked out. The next time any of us attends a meeting, watch to see if the roles are being shared. It's entirely possible that a good meeting can run for its duration with the leader sitting back and apparently doing very little. The best thing for us to do is try it ourselves. If we've been designated as the leader, we accept gladly; but during the meeting we see if we can get others to play the roles we've talked about. We'll probably find that this gets more commitment from the people there.

Let's see how it might go in a meeting. The leader is Doug. The conferees include Debbi, Phil, and Blanche. Others are there, but we won't go into their roles. The meeting has been going on for awhile when we pick it up:

DEBBI: I don't think that's going to work at all. That idea has been tried before.

PHIL: Well, maybe not quite like I suggested. Besides, that was some time ago, and things have changed a lot since then. I think it'll work.

DEBBI: I can't see how. If we go out to the metropolitan offices and make a proposal like that, they'll laugh us out of the place.

BLANCHE: Is there some way we can wrap it in a different wrapper?

PHIL: What do you mean, "a different wrapper"?

BLANCHE: If it's a good idea but people remember the old way we did it, then call it by a different name, use a different approach, give it our endorsement, let people know we've put some thought into it.

PHIL: Well, that seems a little underhanded . . .

DEBBI: Hmm. I see what you're saying, though, Blanche. Really, it isn't the idea that's bad, just the reputation.

BLANCHE: That's right. As I hear you two talking about it, I think it's something that's pretty timely. It would be a shame if we lost the use of the idea just because at another time under different circumstances a similar idea didn't get the job done.

PHIL: I can't argue with that, and there are some changes that must be made. I guess I agree with Debbi that a few of the things I've proposed could be improved on. Why don't we give it a try this way?

DEBBI: If we make the right changes, I think I'll be willing to give my support all the way.

What did we learn? Where was the leader? We never did hear from Doug. Why not? Simple; he wasn't needed. Things were going too' well for him to get in and merely duplicate what the others were doing very well with by themselves. Note that there was some giving in, some compromising, some delving into history, and some negotiating going on. There was a plan of action gradually being developed; and more than anything else, there was some commitment going into the final product of the meeting. This isn't to say that the leader couldn't and indeed shouldn't have stepped in if things had gotten out of control or if there didn't seem to be any direction. But when we have somebody like Blanche doing such a masterful job—perhaps without even consciously thinking about it—we should stay out!

LEADERSHIP ROLES

We've talked a lot about the leadership roles people play. Here's a brief summary of these roles and the part each plays. Think about them the next time a meeting comes along and see if anybody but the leader is playing them. In fact, let's see if we can play some of them when we're not the nominal leader, not to take the role away from the leader but to give all the help we can.

Harmonizer: Keeps the atmosphere friction-free; looks for points of agreement rather than stirring up disagreement. Will recognize supporting statements from different participants and bring them out.

Compromiser: Will work for agreement by using trade-offs. Recognizes when people are willing to give in on certain points and which things they feel strongly about. Serves as moderator in negotiation.

Conscience: Reminds group of the goal and makes effort to keep them moving. May use chastisement to move toward the goal. Expresses discomfort when group is needlessly hung up on unimportant point.

Gatekeeper: Understands the process of moving a group off dead center. Will use techniques of questioning or repetition or reflection to get things going. Knows when group is ready to move to another point.

Catalyst: Asks creative and even uncomfortable questions to get group thinking. Will be able to bring in reticent participants by arousing emotions or getting them involved in one of the issues.

Summarizer: Keeps group aware of where they are. Marks their progress with a summary or feedback on decisions. Recognizes when there is a repetition or discussion on topics already settled and moves group on with a good transition statement. May take notes for group or even work at the flip chart or chalkboard to summarize.

ENDING THE CONFERENCE

Just as it is important to know how to plan, start, and conduct a meeting, it is important to know how and when to end one. Why should this be a particular problem? Isn't everyone anxious to get out of the meeting and back on the job? Yes, probably so, but that's often the trouble. We let them go before we have taken care of some important matters. For example, when it appears we have covered all necessary points and reached the proper solutions, we're ready to adjourn, aren't we? No, not yet! Does the group know what the conclusions are? Do the people know what we and they have agreed to do and say? Do they know who's supposed to do what? These things have to be taken care of or all our efforts may go for naught. Maybe just a summary statement is all we need; "So this is what we've agreed to do: First we will write a memo to our downstate office. . . ." By stating these things clearly and concisely we are asking for commitment and consent. If we have watched the meeting closely, there shouldn't be any misunderstanding; but we state the agreements anyway so there will be no doubts. We also state the action we have planned and who has the responsibility for taking care of the action. We make sure all participants understand their roles and are committed to carrying them out. If another meeting is required or some reporting period is necessary, this should be settled without doubt. If certain people are to finish certain actions before the next meeting, a schedule should be worked out and the timetable agreed upon. If we suspect that one or more of the people don't really know what they're supposed to do or aren't committed to the assignment, this is the time to get it straight. Once the meeting is over, it's going to be difficult to take care of these things.

FOLLOWING UP ON THE MEETING

It would seem that after all that has been done so far to make this a successful meeting, there surely is nothing left to do. Maybe not, but don't be too sure. There are at least three things that need to be done before we can call it a completely successful session. First, we need to check on the action of all those who had things to do and deadlines to meet. Are they staying on schedule? Are they doing what the group at the meeting really decided on? Have they run into problems that were not anticipated? Common sense tells us that we will need to do these things and find the answers to these questions. Second, we should report the action of the conference to those managers and others who need to be advised. The report need not necessarily be a long set of notes or minutes, but it should contain enough information so that those who could not attend or who will be affected by the results will know what was done and what was planned. Finally, we need to take a retrospective look at the meeting in an effort to improve our own ability to conduct meetings. How did we do? Were there things that should have been handled differently? Will we be likely to make the same mistakes again, or do we see how we went wrong? Did we handle the conflict well? Did we recognize the support we were getting from some of the conferees, and did we make use of it? As new supervisors we may make some mistakes in conducting our first meetings; this is expected and acceptable. However, if we don't look at our actions and our mistakes with a view toward doing better the next time, our next mistakes are inexcusable!

CONCLUSION

Someone has described a conference as a "meeting with a purpose." That's as good a definition as we can think of to describe the attitude we should have toward a conference. Some dread going to conferences; some dread conducting them. We should understand that the conference isn't just another meeting with no purpose, but rather a gathering together of specific people for a specific purpose at a specific time. If we can't readily find the purpose of the conference, then by the definition we've just seen it isn't a real conference. It's a purposeless collection of people who waste the organization's time and may make unnecessary decisions about unimportant things. When we put an announced purpose on the gathering, it becomes a full-fledged conference and deserves all the attention we can give it to make it a success. And that's what it takes to make a conference a success—all the attention we can give it. Good conferences aren't measured solely by how well we handled the "talkers" or how close we came to the announced quitting time, but by their results. True, how we handled the conference will have some effect on the results, but there's a lot more to it than that. Results will depend on how well the conference was planned in the first place, how well we did in selecting conferees, and how well we did in sharing the various functions of conference leading. If we ended up playing all the roles from gatekeeper to summarizer we may have had a good conference personally, but it's doubtful that anyone else did.

The logic behind a good conference is pretty simple: "Conference" implies a group of people conferring. The process goes like this. We select some people to come together to confer because a problem exists, and they are the people who are concerned with the problem or have some information that will help in solving that problem. Our job as conference leader is to motivate and direct those people in such a way that there won't be a problem after we've had the conference or after we carry out the action decided on by the people attending. This means that we use these resources skillfully to do what they can do best—solve the problem at hand. If further action is required, we make sure to get their commitment to solve the problem by involving them in both the strategy of problem-solving and the necessary action. As we said in Chapter 6, on planning and organizing, the planning isn't complete until the plan has been acted upon. We should never leave a conference without all participants knowing exactly what is expected of them and when they are to complete what they have agreed to do. Finally, it is important that there be the followup we mentioned. See to it that they do their part. That's our part!

EXERCISES

1. Individual activity: Have each member of the group think of the last meeting he or she went to. Try to pinpoint the date, who attended, and what the purpose was. They should be thinking of an actual meeting, not just remembering in general past meetings they've attended. Once they've picked a specific meeting, they should make a list of the things that helped the meeting to go well, and the things that kept it from running well. They should set up their paper as follows:

Things that helped	Things that hindered
1.	1.
2.	2.
etc.	etc.

2. Group activity: When the individuals have finished Exercise 1, they should report it and have it recorded. This will give rather long lists of things that help and things that hinder the success of a meeting. These lists are valuable, and each person should keep a copy of them for future use. For now, though, let the group decide what the conference or meeting leader could do to overcome the "hindrances" that are listed. Many of them are obvious, like set an agenda, set starting and stopping times, etc. Others are most subtle. These, too, should be listed on the board and made a part of the observers' permanent notes.

3. Group activity: Again looking at the list generated from Exercise 1, have the group discuss how many of the hindrances could have been overcome by the participants, apart from whatever the leader could have done. Brainstorm a list of things participants can do in any meeting to make it better, even if the leader isn't doing a very good job.

4. Individual activity: Each person should think of a meeting he or she will be attending in the near future. It may be a large one or simply a small unit meeting with a few people attending. Take a few minutes and answer the following questions.

What is the purpose of the meeting?

What is the expected product?

Who should attend?

When should they be notified?

How should they be notified?

Are some people more important to the meeting than others?

Is seating arrangement important—and if so, how will they sit?

Can I assign certain leadership roles to some of the people—and if so, to whom?

What time is the meeting scheduled?

What time should it be over?

How much leeway have I got?

(This information need not be fed back to the entire group. Small subgroups can review one another's responses and compare their progress.)

12
PROBLEM-SOLVING

Problem-solving, like most of the other supervisory functions discussed thus far, is a skill. There are specific steps in the process which, when properly followed, almost guarantee success. The difficulty often comes when we start to examine the process in detail, because the steps sound complicated. Actually, the process is simple, and we instinctively use it most of the time in our personal decisions. When we consider buying a car, a house, or a stereo, we go through these steps—not necessarily consciously, but we do use each of them. So as we discuss the steps, it's a good idea to think about how we use them in solving our everyday problems. We can use the process or its steps on big, job-related problems as well as on the small ones that often can grow into big ones if they aren't handled correctly. Also, we can relate the use of problem-solving to our own affairs. For example, we realize that we sometimes have to resort to buying things on credit, and in the process we end up paying more money for them. In the same way the organization which we work for sometimes runs into the same problem—not enough cash to pay now and save money later.

The suggestion here is to start developing the habit of using the specific steps on small items until we automatically go through the steps in any problem situation we face, whatever its size or scope. We will look at the steps, see how they work, give some examples, and leave it up to the supervisor to make the application on his or her own.

DEFINING THE PROBLEM

The first step in problem-solving is to be sure we are attacking the right problem. Suppose a clerk typist comes to us and claims to be tired of working on a certain task. If we take that at face value and immediately start to solve that apparent problem, we may find that we are solving the wrong problem and creating another. In reality, the typist may be frustrated with us as a supervisor, may have had disagreement with the employee who works at the next desk, or may be making more mistakes than necessary because he or she hasn't had enough training.

How can we know if we are trying to solve the right problem? The best approach is to do what the doctor does when examining a patient—get all the symptoms together and see what kind of picture develops. This way we won't be apt to treat a mere symptom, but we can get to the real problem. Once we identify the symptoms, we start to look for the things or events that could produce these symptoms. If employees are doing poor work, that may be a symptom of poor attitudes which in turn may be a symptom of poor supervision or poor working conditions. Are there other corroborative signs, such as high turnover rates, absenteeism, tardiness, etc.? Are some of the employees performing to standard while others aren't? Have these same employees performed better in times past? Only after we have satisfied ourselves with the answers to these questions can we be sure we are solving the correct problem and not just treating a sympton. Once we are sure we know what the problem is, it's a good idea to state it for our own clarification. "Reduce the error rate. Increase the overall production rate for the group." Note that it's not the time to say, "Reduce the error rate caused by the faulty work flow." This assumes that we already know the cause of the problem. That may turn out to be the case, but it's a good idea to get a few more facts before identifying the cause. This brings us to the next step in the problem-solving process.

GATHERING INFORMATION

The information stage is an important one, but it's one that's often taken lightly. After we've spent this time defining the problem, don't we have enough information? No, not at this stage; we aren't ready to solve the problem yet. We just want to get as much information as we can to help us be sure we really are solving the right problem, this information will also help us generate some ideas on how to solve the problem. Once we've gathered as many facts as seem to be available in the time we have to look, we take one last look to see if we really are on the right track. Have we discovered that every supervisor before us has had the same tardiness problem with the same employees on the same job? This doesn't make the problem go away, but it does change its complexion.

Note that we emphasized getting as many facts as time allows.

One of the important decisions that supervisors must be able to make is to know when to stop looking and start solving. In other words, we must recognize the point at which going further would take more time and effort than the problem deserves. We might like to have computer error records for the three previous years; but if such information would take weeks of digging by a number of employees, we need instinctively to be able to measure its value against the cost of obtaining it. On the other hand, if the information is readily available in the files, we can't use the tired excuse, "It'll take too long to get the information." Note, again, we aren't yet looking for a solution, and any information should be gathered with an open mind. It would be self-deluding for us to gather only that information that will help us prove a point rather than solve the real problem. If we go into the problem-solving process with preconceived notions of what we are going to do anyway, then following specific procedures is often mere wasted motion.

During this information-gathering stage it is essential for us to get specific, "hard" information rather than generalities. We need to find out things like who or what, how many, how much, where, when, how long, etc. We will find this kind of information harder to get than general comments, but it will be much more reliable and useful in the long run. For example, it's not enough to have statements like, "She's late all the time." We need to ask, "How many times in the last month?" We shouldn't accept information like, "This mailing machine is costing us a fortune in repair bills." Such shaky information could sink our argument and in the process embarrass us one of these days. If we don't ask it, our boss might: "How much is a fortune?" Admittedly, generalities and opinions are much easier to get; and we probably make more friends and admirers when we ask their opinions instead of making them dig up specific information. But we are trying to solve a specific problem for which, hopefully, we are going to recommend some specific action. If all of this is based only on opinions, we aren't likely to have the best solution available. By the way, when we're getting this information, we should make some kind of mental or written note on just how reliable the information really is. If some information is questionable, we should so note it; otherwise we may find ourselves making decisions on that information just as if it were completely reliable. If we know that there is some doubt as to the validity of the information, we'll treat it with sufficient caution later on. If not, we may forget and later create for ourselves and others frustration and embarrassment that could easily have been avoided.

FINDING THE CAUSE

At this point we still aren't ready for the solution, but we are ready to identify the cause. Only after we have found the cause can we select an appropriate solution. Using the information we have gathered, we look at all the possible causes. If we decide that the cause of the poor work output is inadequate training—that it is not poor work habits—then we have some valuable data to use toward applying the proper solution. However, we may find that we will need more information or a different kind of information to pinpoint and to address the cause.

The difficult thing to remember is that causes aren't always easy to identify. Rather than say that the cause isn't obvious, we should say the cause that is obvious may not be the real problem. If we have a problem because one of the employees in the office is being abrupt with people in other departments, the cause may not be his or her bad attitude. It may be that we haven't made the assignment to cooperate completely clear. An employee who is afraid that the job he or she has is not as important as other jobs will often do his or her best to make it seem it is, even if the attempt irritates other people. "I'm sorry, but I'm too busy to help with the address changes right now." "Did the boss tell you to handle that rate revision memo?" "That's my job and I don't want you causing me problems later." The cause of the statements may be poor supervision on our part, poor definition of work responsibility, inadequate work, or several other things. But if we've gotten enough information, we should have a reasonable idea at this stage just what the real cause of the problem is.

After we are sure we have the cause isolated, it's still a good idea to make a quick check of past history. For example, did the switch to an automated billing system cause the same problem at some other department or office? Has this same problem been caused before by a changeover to new policy forms? Have we always had this problem when we put in new photocopy equipment? There are several good reasons for checking past history for cases where we have identified the cause. First, has someone identified the cause of this problem before and tried to solve it by eliminating the cause? Did the problem go away? Did the solution turn out to be more expensive than it was worth? Did it turn out to be only part of the solution? Are the basic ingredients—the same staff, the same office layout, the same equipment— still there? If they are, did the solution just fail to take effect, or has some new ingredient or variable entered the picture?

The second good reason for checking history is to find out if there is any record of the problem going away by itself. Some problems are that way. With a change in the office routine trouble develops, and we intuitively know we should do something but aren't sure just what. Then before we know it, the problem has disappeared! The danger in this kind of thinking is that most of us tend to generalize incorrectly that all problems will go away sooner or later. This just isn't so. Many potentially good supervisors have fallen by the wayside waiting for the problems to disappear. Even many problems that seem to leave come back later in another form, often much more complex and formidable; so we can't wait just because some problems do go away. But we can find out if this particular problem is caused by a particular thing that has a history of repeating itself, then going away. For example, when it's time to replace a typewriter in the office, we can be sure that there will be someone who isn't happy with your selection of who gets the new one, no matter how fair your decision is. A check with experienced supervisors may tell us what to expect when the new-typewriter decision is made. This same check may tell us that some of the employees will probably be miffed; they always are, but it will probably wear off by itself. If we are satisfied that this is right and that the new typewriter caused the problem, we can be equally satisfied that time will heal the problem just as well as any other solution we pick. Of course, if we know enough about the situation before we select the person who gets the new typewriter, we may do some things to keep the problem from arising.

FINDING ALTERNATIVE SOLUTIONS

Now comes the tricky stage where we have already determined the cause and are going to try to find the best solution to eliminate whatever is causing the problem. The reason this is tricky is that it is the last time in the process we can really use much imagination or ingenuity. What we want to do now is to think of several possible solutions. We want the best one, and there is a way of getting it. The process is to brainstorm—think of as many alternatives or options as possible without making any efforts to evaluate them, or decide on one, or throw any of them out as not being feasible. The most important thing is that we must not allow ourselves to think, "Well, I'm sure that won't work, so I'll rule it out now." About the only rule is to concentrate on those solutions that will most likely remove the cause we have located. If there is doubt, keep the idea around anyway unless the doubt is very strong. We might even ask ourselves, "Why did I think of this in the first place? There must be some reason it came to mind, so I'd better keep it for awhile."

The problem with evaluating too early is that we may overlook some potentially good ideas by just not getting around to thinking about them! We hit on an idea that sounds good and we go with it and never even think of alternatives that may have been better in the long run. To make it worse, the idea we picked to solve our problem may end up being less effective than we hoped, either because it turned out to have some flaws in it or because it wasn't as practical as it sounded to us in the beginning. By the time we find it out, we may have used up too much time or gone too far to consider other options. We may even find ourselves committed to this solution and have to support it, knowing it isn't the best possible answer to our problem.

After we have spent some time listing, either mentally or on paper, all the ideas that we can think of, we should take a last look at them to see if anything else comes to mind. This will tell us if we've paid too much attention to a single line of thought. Often ideas cause us to think of other ideas, so the time may be well spent. This is also a good time to ask, "How do I know when I have enough options to choose from?" The answer is that we have to look at the problem and decide how much time it's worth. The bigger or more complex the problem, the more time and other resources can be devoted to solving it. Two things are sure: We can spend too much time looking for more alternatives; and we can be pretty sure that we will reach the saturation point on productive ideas after awhile. In other words, we reach a point of diminishing returns where the same amount of time no longer produces the same quality of alternative.

An advantage of listing the options we have looked at is that at some point when we are trying to justify the solution we chose, we can say, "Well, I considered these other options but this is why I chose this one." If we have done a good job of thinking out our decisions, we can show why the alternative we chose is better than the ones we rejected. Of course, if for some reason there is a need to take one of the other options (company policy, budget consideration, increasing computerization, etc.), then it's also important to be able to say, "I considered that also; and if we go that route, here are the things that will have to be done . . . ." A final advantage is that it's sometimes possible to sell an idea by showing what the alternatives are. If someone doesn't like what we have chosen, it's good to be able to say that the alternatives are thus and so. It's a lot better for us to list the options first than for someone else to ask, "Why haven't you considered . . .?" It weakens our decisions and credibility if we have to say that there are things we haven't considered, even if they turn out later to be bad alternatives.

PICKING A SOLUTION

Now that we've gone through all of this logic, how do we next go about picking the best solution from the options we have listed? There are some definite steps, and we need to consider them now. We need to use a systematic approach. It would be counterproductive to go this far in such a careful manner and then lose all of the advantage by not using the same disciplined approach in picking the best alternative. The approach should be a screening process to examine each of the options we have picked to determine if they meet certain criteria. If so, we can use them; if not, we can begin to eliminate them one by one.

First, we ask ourselves if the alternative we are looking for is really possible. We said earlier that we didn't want to rule out any ideas at that point, but now we begin to be deliberately critical and evaluative. Now is the time to decide whether or not the idea really will work. Is it within the capability of our department, our technical talents, and our budget? Next, we ask ourselves if the alternative is really workable. Even if we have the capabilities, will it work under the real-world conditions that exist in our work situation? Will our clerical and technical employees accept the idea? Will this option fit into our organization's way of doing things., considering how responsive our systems are, how conveniently we join with upstream or downstream work groups, etc? Then we ask ourselves if the alternative we are considering is really a probable solution. Are we ready to use it; are we willing to stick our necks out and pull for this as a solution? Will our manager accept the idea? What is the probability that the idea will work and will be used? Finally, we ask the key question: Is the idea applicable to this problem at this time under these circumstances?

This last question is the most critical of all. We must be sure that the solution applies to the real problem—the one we finally settled on in the beginning. As we study the alternative to see whether or not to use it, we want to know not only if it applies to the specific problem but also if it solves all of it? We should be comfortable with an alternative that gets this far in the testing sequence, and we will be if we are sure it fits the problem and will solve all of it because of the systematic approach we have used. We have eliminated most of the poorer solutions by now. The way to evaluate the ones that are left is to put them to one more test. We have, of course, placed certain "must" conditions on each of these solutions, and any option we picked had to meet these "musts". But as a consequence, we find that they also meet certain "nice" conditions, some more than others. We have said that we realize we can't expect everything, but there are things that would be nice to have while we are using the option we chose. Once we have found those that get this far, one way to pick the best alternative is to look carefully at the "nice" benefits we get from each one. Those that meet all of the "musts" and provide the most or best "nice" items become the most attractive to us, and it is from this list that we pick the final solution. Stated simply, we pick the one that not only will solve the problem we have stated, but will also give us the best side benefits. We have to be careful here, though, because we don't want to become attached to an idea just for its side benefits. Because of some side benefit we feel so strongly about, we could end up defending a solution beyond its merit when another option might solve the problem just as well, be more popular with other people, and perhaps be the most practical one to pick.

Once we have chosen an alternative and it has been checked out according to the suggestions here, we need to state it clearly. For the benefit of all concerned we should make sure that everyone who hears about the solution knows exactly who is going to do what and what it will take in terms of people, money and time. If we have decided to move certain employees into a new workflow, we should specify which employees, where they will be placed, and what their job responsibilities will be when they are in the new work situation. If we have decided to go into overtime, we should state how much overtime will be required, who will work it, and how much it will cost. Remember, early in this chapter we said that this could sound complicated but that it really isn't. Once those concerned have been told, the information should simply be available if someone asks. It can be summarized in our minds if we have thought out the problem thoroughly.

PUTTING THE PLAN TO WORK

We have now come to the point of implementing the solution. How do we go about introducing the new idea? This shouldn't be a problem but it often is, and many plans fall through at this point. Again, certain questions must be asked. We have to anticipate problems and try to decide ahead of time how we will handle them. For example, we should

ask ourselves, "Who will be likely to resist this solution?" If we anticipate that one of the senior clerical employees will try to kill the idea,
we should take steps to prevent this, even if it means going to that
employee and getting him or her to help introduce it or to give us
some suggestions on ways to make it work. We need to decide what
risks are involved in trying this new or different idea and who will
likely misunderstand what we are trying to do. Is our own manager in
agreement? Will he or she back us up when implementation questions
arise or opposition appears? After we've tried to anticipate who will
be affected and what problems this will cause, we should see if all risks,
resistance, and resentments are covered. If they are, it's time to carry
out the plan we've chosen, but before we do that, we need to assure
ourselves that we know what we're talking about.

Going through these steps one more time should give us the confidence to go ahead with the solution to the problem. We mention this
now for two reasons: First, as new supervisors, we aren't always
accepted for what we know or do. We are still thought of as new and
thus not capable of thinking as effectively as others with more time and
experience. Though this isn' true, it doesn't keep people from feeling
that way; so it has to be considered. Second, we should not be afraid
to press our ideas. By going through the steps we've discussed we have
become very familiar not only with the problem but also with the
alternatives for solving it. In a way we have become experts on this
small portion of the operation, and this should overcome the lack of
confidence that others have in us and that we have in ourselves. This
"set" of mind is important to the outcome of the project! Now comes
the critical part of making our plan operate. We have spent valuable
time arriving at what we think is the best solution to the problem; we
have confidence that it is going to work; but it won't work by itself!
If the plan is poorly carried out the results can make the solution look
like the wrong one, even it it's right. Surely the solution deserves as
much careful attention in the doing stage as it did in the selection and
planning stage.

Carrying out the plan means more than just putting it to work or
telling someone else to do the job. It means keeping track of the progress, watching how well things are going, and even making adjustments
along the way. We must be careful to avoid being so committed to the
plan that we can't see things that are going wrong. Our commitment
should be to the job, not our plan. This doesn't mean that we have
to spend time nervously watching everything that happens. If we have
confidence in the plan, we should be able to let it run its course.

Occasional spot checking should tell us if we are really solving the problem. If we have reassigned some of the employees to different jobs or tasks, then we can tell a great deal by looking at relevant data through sampling. If we have made changes in procedures, then occasionally checking the present results with previous ones will tell us what we need to know about the plan we are implementing.

While we are monitoring the plan in operation, it's a good idea to keep an eye out for potential trouble. We've already talked about making a mental or written note on where we might expect opposition or misunderstanding. Since we know this ahead of time, we have some good check points. The key is to know when trouble is brewing so we can head it off rather than waiting until things are in bad shape to step in. The skill of anticipating trouble is a difficult but valuable one to learn. Most trouble can be stopped more easily when it first starts than after it's gone on awhile. If we suspect that someone is going to misunderstand or not like the solution we are instituting, we'd better make sure that they don't get too many opinions formed before we deal with their misunderstandings. It will be a lot harder to change their minds than it will be to help them make up their minds in the first place.

Part of the reason for watching the progress of our solution is to check on our own problem-solving ability. Sometime in the future we will need to know just how well we did at defining the problem, selecting alternatives, and picking the right option. Not only will we want to know how well we did at this but we will also want to get a look at the value of the solution. As we think about our future problem-solving efforts, we will want to ask ourselves, "Was all of this done efficiently, or did I spend a lot of time coming up with a solution that is now falling apart at the seams? What kind of job did I do in anticipating where the trouble would come from?" All of this leads us to the final step of following up on the solution after the plan has been put to work.

FOLLOWING UP ON THE SOLUTION

The basic question we now ask is, "Did the solution really work?" The answer will tell us most of what we want to know. No matter how well thought out the plan was or how well we implemented it, if it didn't solve the problem, it wasn't very effective. But if it worked and we got at least some of the side benefits we anticipated, then the solution was a good one. If possible, we should try to find out why the solution worked. This may seem redundant, but there is always the possibility that the problem disappeared in spite of what we did rather than because of it. This means that we try to determine if there were other factors at work at the same time which may have had an effect on the outcome of the problem-solving effort. While this isn't worth an exorbitant amount of time, it's worth at least some to keep us from believing we have solved a problem by ourselves when in fact some other factor has as much to do with the outcome as what we did.

As we cautioned earlier, we should always be alert to flaws in the solution. How could we have avoided the negative results that happened? Were there obvious prior signs that we missed, or was the error unavoidable? Would it have been worth the extra time to look longer for possible trouble? Admittedly this is hindsight, but it's valuable. It can help us avoid making the same mistakes later; it can help us measure our own ability at problem-solving. It can be of help to future problem-solvers in our department; because if we have a good idea of what happened, they can learn from both our successes and our failures. Of course, all of this presupposes that the problem is dead, not just dormant. Sometimes problems disappear for awhile just because we have done something different; but as soon as things settle down, they reappear.

Part of following up on the solution includes finding out exactly how much it took in resources to make the solution work. How much did it really cost? How much overtime did we put in that was directly related to our solution? Is the job now more complicated as a result of our action? These are fair questions to ask, and we may well need the information to support our next idea. If we have exceeded our estimated expenditure, it's a lot better for us to catch it than for someone else to. Also, when we find out exactly what the costs were in terms of money, material, and people, we can honestly answer the question, "Was it worth it?" This can be done only when all the facts and figures are in.

CONCLUSION

In the beginning of this chapter we said that the process appears complicated at first. We have tried to give the complete sequence of steps for an approach to problem-solving. It will be rare when we use each of these steps to its full extent, but the idea is to realize that the approach to problem-solving is systematic and not haphazard. Breaking it down into steps, as we have done here, shows clearly that there is a beginning, a middle, and an end. The middle is only the one step of picking a solution. What comes before and after determines how well the solution we pick is going to work. Briefly, here are the steps as they have been given:

1. Defining the problem (Example: Our clerical turnover is too high compared to previous periods.)

2. Gathering information (Example: We have reduced the training time; we have more trainees than in previous periods).

3. Finding the cause (Example: We determine that the reduced and haphazard training time is the cause.)

4. Finding alternative solutions (Example: Have new employees train for two hours a day for the first 10 days on the job or have the employees receive three solid days of training before actually starting real work.)

5. Picking a solution (Example: We pick the first of the above because of practicality and affordability. We assign our best trainer(s) to the training assignment.)

6. Putting the plan to work (Example: We do the training ourselves or carefully monitor whoever does it to see that they follow prescribed steps, procedures, time, etc.)

7. Carrying out the plan (Example: We monitor systematically to determine how the employees apply what they've learned to the actual job or task.)

8. Following up on the solution (Example: We compare data before and after to determine the cost/benefit.)

We should write these down and paste them somewhere around our desk. When we start to solve a problem, we can review the list and ask, "Where am I right now in the problem-solving process?" If we can't decide where we are, we'd better question our solution. If we're lucky or just happen to be doing a good job, we can find out where we are in the process and continue, assured that we're heading down the right road.

EXERCISES

1. Subgroup activity: Using the steps in problem-solving shown at the end of this chapter, go through the following problem, working in small groups of no more than four people.

Bill Jackson is an accountant in a western state who for some time has been keeping books for medium and small business and doing tax returns. Next Saturday he has a chance to do a job in a distant city which is a drive of about 70 miles. The Jacksons have two cars, one with automatic shift and the other with a standard shift. His wife Betty never learned to drive a standard shift, so she drives the automatic and he drives the standard. The standard needs new tires for road driving; but the old ones still have "in town" miles left on them. The automatic has new tires but they won't fit on the standard. It is Thursday when Bill finds out about the job in the distant city. When he calls his wife to tell her about it, he asks her what, if anything, she has planned for Saturday. Her reply is that she plans to take the new neighbor, Sally Thorne, shopping.

At this point we'll stop and let the subgroups work on the problem. When each group is finished, someone should read out it's answers to the entire group. A record of the answers should be kept.

2. Group activity: Using the same information as above, determine what we don't know in order to solve the problem adequately. How much information would be required to actually solve the problem? Suppose we were to find out that Sally Thorne doesn't have a car. Would this help us? And suppose we find out that the local bus doesn't go to the shopping center on Saturday? We still don't have all the information. What is needed? Have the group brainstorm exactly what we need to know in order to bring the problem to an adequate conclusion. (It's interesting how many might have suggested going ahead and buying the tires for the other car as a solution. While this has some merit, it's the kind of thing we do often in problem-solving if we don't have all the information we need—which many times is the case!).

13
ORAL AND WRITTEN PRESENTATIONS

As supervisors we find ourselves having to present solutions to problems we have solved or communicate our ideas up or down the line. We may do this either orally or in writing. In either case, the acceptance of the message can depend as much on the quality of our writing or speaking as on the message itself. It's unfortunate that we sometimes lose an argument or get poor results because we fail to do well at either putting it in writing or speaking directly to people. Obviously we can't become accomplished writers or speakers by reading one chapter in a book, but we can step back and think through what we should be trying to do when we write or speak. Before going further, though, it would be a good idea to review the chapter on communications (Chapter 5), because we will need to apply some of the basics of communications in order to understand and implement what is said here.

WATCH STEREOTYPES

Perhaps the most common mistake we make in trying to improve our writing or speaking is to assume that there is just one right way to write or speak. We fail to realize that there are many acceptable ways to express ourselves. In writing we can reach our audience by saying what we say in several ways that are quite acceptable. Not realizing that anyone who says there is only one way to set up a letter is misinformed, we search for the perfectly correct form to use in writing a letter. The fact is that if we stick to some kind of stereotyped form in expressing our thoughts, we may be stereotyping ourselves. We may be saying that we have no imagination, or that we are stiff and aloof even when the occasion calls for an informal approach. We may be giving the impression that we are old-fashioned and that we lack the adaptability required to suit a particular situation. Whether we're speaking or writing, there is plenty of room for imaginative individuality, which means that the person who always says something in a stylized way or appears to be the perfect platform orator may not be the best communicator. In fact, the polished orator will probably be out of place in the kind of speaking situations the supervisor is placed in. There is really one basic standard for writing or speaking: *Get the message across.*

There is a three-point plan of action that consistently works well. If we know these three things, we should be able to meet any kind of situation in which we are trying to get a message to someone else, whether by speaking or writing. They are:

1. Know your subject.
2. Know your audience.
3. Know your own capabilities.

Let's look at each and see what it means to us as supervisors.

Know your subject

What does it mean to know the subject? It means that we should research it until we are sure we have a solid understanding of what we are about to communicate. Even if we aren't supposed to be experts, we should at least know enough to see that our words and phrases are used correctly. This doesn't mean that we over-research the topic, but it does mean that we learn as much as we are supposed to know plus perhaps a little extra—never a little less. Of course, if we are regarded as a bona fide expert and others are looking to us for the answers, then we do, in fact, have to do a great deal of research. Perhaps a practical criterion is to know what is important and what isn't. Rather than becoming an expert on a whole subject, we determine what part is important to the audience or the reader and concentrate on that. We may even have to persuade and educate the audience to the fact that certain things are important. We also think through what part is important to the project we're working on. Maybe the audience is interested in more information than the project requires; maybe they think it would be interesting to pursue some aspects that really aren't pertinent to solving the problem at hand or that do not contribute to the overall project. If so, we simply have to sidestep the irrelevant material and get to the important points, even though our audience thinks it wants something else. This means we must explain why we are leaving things out and be ready to defend our position. But the audience isn't the only reason we add to the information we cover. We have our own pet subjects that we like to elaborate on every time we get a chance, so we have to control ourselves as well.

One good way to regulate ourselves and our audience is to be familiar with the subjects that relate to the one we're writing or speaking about. We don't have to become experts but we need enough knowledge to tell how some of the related material might affect the outcome of the project being discussed and be able to answer some of the questions that might be asked later. We shouldn't pose as an expert or try to bluff on the subject. We should simply try to familiarize ourselves with enough of the information to give us a pretty good picture of those factors that relate to the subject at hand. Later on, as we grow, we can take on more related subjects; but in the beginning it's better to be good at what we're talking about than to try to spread ourselves too thin. Organization is the key here, because as we begin to organize and close up loose ends, we see where related subjects fit in and where the weak spots are.

Know your audience

Knowing the audience isn't as simple as it might appear. As we've already said, if we want them to have different information from what they think they need, then we must tell them in terms that are meaningful to them. Even though we're expressing our own thoughts and ideas on the subject, the way we express them must be understandable to our audience. Ideally, we should start off by making it clear that what the audience is getting is what it has asked for. This way at least the members are tuned in, whether they're getting the information exactly as they expected it or not. The way to appeal to the reader or listener is the same: "Here is the information you asked for." "You asked me to speak on. . . ." At least we ought to start by saying, "You will be glad to know. . . ." Whatever we do, we should use the name of our reader or listener, and second person, rather than "I" or "me". This helps keep it friendly, especially if we avoid stock phrases such as, "Enclosed please find. . . ." Using phrases like this may say something about us that we don't want said. Remember that stopping is just as important as starting. Nothing can be kinder or friendlier than stopping when we have said all we have to say; but if we aren't careful, we fall back into some bad habits which often kill whatever good might have been accomplished.

Know your own capabilities

The most important thing to know is ourselves. What are our capabilities? If we have the ability to talk and write on a subject, we shouldn't sell ourselves short. It's reason enough to write or speak because we know enough about the subject to do just that. We also have a chance to sell ourselves, and to prove a point that we've come up with, and these are opportunities we should take advantage of. We may have a solution or an idea; and if we have done the research, we should not be willing to let someone else try to explain it just because we think we lack the ability to do so. It's often true that good ideas go down the drain because we fail to take advantage of the opportunity to sell them ourselves. We either let the idea go altogether or entrust it to someone else who may lack the whole story or the interest to sell it.

Of course, we also need to know our limitations; and even if we are willing to make the speech or write the letter, we should speak or write within our abilities. If we can't tell jokes, we shouldn't try. Instead use a substitute, such as a short anecdote from the newspaper, or just play it straight—that nearly always works! If we can't be an orator, we shouldn't try. We should tell it simply and quickly and stop when we're through. If we aren't familiar with certain words or phrases, we leave them alone. We're better off not using them than using them incorrectly. And if we aren't sure about them, what about our audience? Just as we need to know our limitations, we also need to do something about them. We should be constantly striving to do better than the last time. Each time we write or speak, it's a good idea to add one new challenge; and when someone says, "You did a fine job," determine to do even better next time. If we feel we didn't do too well we don't stop with a failure; we should decide what we did wrong and look for an opportunity to try to do better.

Note that skillful communication is important to the new supervisor. The ability to express oneself in writing or by speaking before a group is an asset that is always useful to anyone in management. At every level in the organization we are called upon to tell someone something. The telling is just as important as the knowing what to tell. Very few things will call attention to us and to what we know like the ability to say it or write it. A good oral briefing or a crisp, accurate report is a precious commodity to those who are short on time and need to get their facts in a hurry; and if we are able to provide them with this service, we will certainly be rewarded for it. The higher we go in the organization, the more useful this skill becomes; so the better we get, the more we improve our likelihood of going higher up. Chances are pretty good that whenever two near-equals are being considered for a job, the one who can communicate better will win out.

TIPS ON WRITING

Generally there are three reasons why we ever write anything: to inform, to request, and to substantiate or document.

1. When we write to inform, we are doing so because someone needs some information we have and has asked us to supply it, or we have some information they should be using and we want them to have it. As we mentioned earlier, they may not know they need it and we may have to persuade them to accept it; but at least we need to recognize that a particular letter is for the purpose of giving someone some information.

2. Writing to request information is different from writing to give information. Our approach is different in that we have to be much more specific to be sure to get just what we need. Even in requesting information there are two reasons why we want it. First, we want it because we are going to use it; second, we want it because someone, perhaps our manager, has asked us to get it. In the first case, we have only to determine exactly what we want and why we want it, then ask for it. In the second case, it's a little more subtle; we have a communications problem at both ends. We not only have to evaluate someone else's needs and make sure we aren't asking for the wrong thing, but we also have to be sure we are getting it in communicable, usable form. This means we have the problem of deciding what the users are going to do with the information. If they are going to use it pretty much as we get it and put it into their report, then we must give it to them in as near final or usable form as possible. If they're going to extract parts of the information and perhaps combine it with other information, then we need to present it in a form that allows them to find specific things quickly. We have another communications challenge in the responsibility of communicating this need to the people we are getting the information from.

3. When writing to substantiate or document a conclusion or decision we have made we have to use all the rules of good communication because we may be assuming a persuading or selling role. This is especially true if we are writing to substantiate someone else's

idea or conclusion, such as when the department or branch manager tells us to, "Write a letter to Jim and tell him what we have decided on this group life insurance risk."

It's usually pretty simple to determine which of the three reasons we are writing for, but often we forget to do it. It's easier to find the right words if we know why we are writing, and it's also easier to proofread our writing when we know exactly why we're writing in the first place. We say to ourselves, "Did I make it perfectly clear what I wanted, or does the downstate branch manager have to guess and read between the lines? Did I spend so much time leading up to the subject that I lost the reason for writing." It's always good to put ourselves in the reader's shoes to see if from that viewpoint we can decide what the letter or report is all about. The simplest way to check our writing is to see if we got to the point quickly. It's just as bad to communicate too much detailed background information as it is to put in too little. If we spend too much time leading up to the reason for writing, the reader may have left us mentally before we get to it. The best way is to open with the purpose of the letter:

"Here's the answer on the loss ratio report you asked for. . . ."

"Can you tell us how many actuarial trainees you will need in the next three years?"

"We recommend modifying the (work measurement) project immediately. . . ."

With such lead-in sentences, the reader won't have to guess why we're writing; but this doesn't mean we should be blunt or tactless, just straightforward and direct.

We get to the point clearly and spare the details until we have established our reason for writing. When we state the purpose early, we don't inadvertently bury it in the third paragraph somewhere between background detail and supplementary information. We don't use obscure or technical words or phrases when they are inappropriate. Also remember that the reader should be able to tell at a glance what he or she is supposed to do.

"Will you send me five copies of the agent's ordinary life sales results?"

"Wait until Friday; I'll call you about the loss prevention conference then."

"Take the necessary steps to purchase that desk calculator we discussed."

All of this comes clearly and early in the report. Any supporting data can come at the end or as an attachment.

Finally, here's a tip that's helpful; to learn to write, we must write! We must practice, reread whatever we've written that didn't get the message across, then practice writing some more. We should read and analyze writings and reports from peers, employees, and clients. We should take them apart, ask ourselves why they worked them as they did, recognize the good things they have done, and then imitate those good things. Most good writers freely admit they started out by imitating people who were already successful, so there's no shame in recognizing and copying good writing style. If there are people in the company or organization who have the reputation for good writing, study what they've written to see what it is that makes their material precise or easy to read, and then try to do likewise.

TIPS ON SPEAKING

One can't learn to speak well merely by reading about it, but there are some points to look for that will improve our ability as speakers if we take advantage of the knowledge we've gained. All of the earlier suggestions about preparation obviously apply here, and much of the success or failure of our speech or presentation will be determined by how well we have done these steps. But even the best preparation won't make competent speakers out of us. We must learn to practice, practice, practice. We don't have to practice every word we're going to say, but we need to work on phrases and try different combinations of words in order to get the most out of them. Since we're more likely to be frightened at the beginning, we should practice our opening remarks until they're as precise and clear as we can make them. If we make a good start, the rest will come easier; our confidence will be higher and the audience reception will be better.

Another way to build confidence is to try out our ideas on other people. We shouldn't bore them or ask them to listen to the entire speech, but at least try to get them to react to our key points and ideas. Do they understand what we're trying to say? Do they see the logic we're using? Do they have some pretty good arguments for why we should say it differently?

When we start to speak, we must be alert to the audience's reaction. Do they look receptive? Are they bored? Is there anyone in the group that looks friendly and appears to be nodding agreement? If so, it will build our confidence to direct our attention to him or her frequently to see how we're doing. Be careful, though; this person may not be a good gauge of the thinking and feeling of the entire audience. One way to keep the audience with us is to get feedback from them. Look them in the eye when we've made a good point and try to get them to nod, smile, or frown. Don't be afraid to ask them to hold up their hands if they are on one side or the other of a question. This way we've made it clear that we're talking to and with them, not at them. Since we want to talk to them, we look at them, not the ceiling, the floor, or our notes. Look around the group; don't talk to just one side of the room or to a few people on the front row.

There's nothing wrong with using notes—in fact, the audience expects it; but we need to use them well or not at all. Notes are just that—notes. They're not our speech written out. Very few people can write out their whole speech and then make it appear casual and natural. Certainly we can't do it if we are just beginning to learn to speak, so it's all the more important for us to make good use of notes. But if our notes are not much shorter than the speech, then we're really just going to end up reading the speech. The rule for making notes is to put only the key points and phrases on them, plus any statistics or figures we need to remember. Again, practice will reduce the need for notes.

One thing that will help us eliminate overdependence on notes is to have some good speaking aids. This introduces another dimension to our speaking that can be misused if we're not careful. We tend to use things such as visuals, charts, chalkboards, or easels as crutches rather than as aids. We depend on them to help us, not the audience. Just because we project many figures on an overhead projector doesn't mean the audience is going to remember it all or even give it their attention for very long. There's hardly any better way to show a relationship of parts to the whole than to use a pie chart or similar "whole" type of graph. We remember what we see much longer than what we hear, so good visuals are necessary to aid in retention. Also visuals can save us words if we use them at the proper time and in the proper way. For example, it would take a lot of words to describe a paint-spraying insurance risk, but a picture could get the message across in a hurry! One consideration is that if we decide to use a visual and think it will aid the audience in getting the message, we should make sure the audience can see the visual. The audience isn't likely to be very receptive when we say, "If you could see this computer form, you'd note that it has thirty-six lines."

CONCLUSION

A final tip for those of us who find ourselves in the situation of having to write something or speak before a group of any size: Be friendly on purpose. Write and speak with a smile. Let our writing show we are friendly by our use of personal pronouns and people's names. Refer to things that the readers are familiar with rather than using examples that relate only to our experience. The same is true for our speaking; pleasantness is contagious. We can become uncommonly effective by communicating our message in a friendly way. This will evolve as we speak and write more and more; and we should try to speak and write more and more. To do our job well, we must steadily develop this communication aspect of it. There are many books written on the subject and many programs of self-help available. We need to take advantage of them as well as to practice by accepting every opportunity to write and speak that we get. If we do poorly, it's a sign that we need practice, not a signal to give up. If we do well, and we will if we keep trying, then we will be more likely to sell our ideas and ourselves.

EXERCISES

1. Individual activity: Each person in the group should write a memorandum to his or her manager about the activity engaged in so far in the study of this book. It should be no longer than 50 words and no more than two paragraphs. It may be edited and doesn't have to be copied over. When all are finished, they should be ready to read their memos to the rest of the group or to others in the group.

2. Small-group activity: Form subgroups of no more than four people. Let each person read his or her memo to the other members of the subgroup. Those members should look for unnecessarily long paragraphs, cumbersome, stilted words, and unimaginative phrases. When all the memos have been read by their writers and comments have been made by the rest of the subgroup, each person should take at least five minutes to redo his or her memorandum.

3. Individual activity: Let each person count the number of words in the memo he or she wrote for Exercise 1, then do the same for the memo written in Exercise 2. Then have each subtract the smaller number from the larger. If the result shows that the second memo had fewer words than the first one, put a plus sign in front of the

result because that's a step forward. If it shows that the second memo had more words than the first, put a minus sign in front of the result because that's a step backward. The idea is to see how many words have been saved in the rewriting. The whole group might read out their results so that a total for the group can be obtained. (The object is to show that if these people can save this many words in writing only a 50-word memorandum, think what they'll do day after day in writing letters and reports if they learn the lesson from this chapter!)

4. Group activity: Brainstorm a presentation that this group might make on how to save words and make the meanings clearer in their writing. This will be an oral presentation. Using the rules of good speaking, decide what the opening remarks should be, how attention can be obtained, and what illustrations should be included. The body of the speech should be outlined, showing the points to be made, and the suggested action or recommendation should be close to the end. The conclusion should be emphatic and dramatic. It should be acted out, with the entire group developing a closing sentence for the speech. While the speech may not be given, it's a good review and can possibly furnish material to someone who wants to pursue the subject further.

14
SELF DEVELOPMENT
AND EVALUATION

It would be convenient to end the book at this point with a few words of exhortation about personal growth and development. But new supervisors need to know how and where to develop themselves. As we get involved in the everyday problems of the job, we forget to look at ourselves to see if we are improving our supervisory skill. We may even forget what areas we are supposed to improve in. Little problems can seem like big ones when they are with us, so we spend our time worrying about them and fail to realize that good supervisors must think about the future as well as the present. Not only do we need to be alert to the long-range objectives of the organization, but we also need to think about some long-range objectives for ourselves. This isn't to say that we should spend all our time worrying about the next job in the hierarchy or our "big promotion," but we have to accept the fact that we aren't going to be of much value to ourselves or the organization if we fail to grow to our full career potential. But how do we develop ourselves and what are the areas that get first attention? The answers to these questions can make the difference in where we will be and what we will be doing 10 years from now.

HOW DO WE DEVELOP?

How can we improve ourselves if we have all the problems of the job to worry about? The chances are we are going to be so busy that we can't take time out to train ourselves or do much planning about the future. This may be the first indicator that we need some development. If we can't get the job done in the time alloted to us and still find some time to look to next week and next year, we may need to evaluate the way we are doing our job. Are we organized in our work effort? Are we spinning our wheels doing things that should be delegated to our clerical or technical staffers? Are we doing things over needlessly because we aren't doing them right the first time? Are we spending too much time on small, insignificant technical details, thereby letting the "people" problems get bigger and bigger? There are some good warning signs to look for to monitor how well we're doing. Let's see what we can do about some of them.

First, consider the matter of not having enough time. One sign that we aren't making the most of our efforts is that we're working without taking time to plan. It's a vicious cycle because the less time we have, the less we plan, and the less we plan, the more time it takes to do the job—so we run out of time. This mushrooms until finally we discover ourselves swamped with work and no time to plan it. The results are that we don't do an efficient job of what we do and may even overlook doing things that should be done. How do we get out of such a dilemma? One way is to turn the process around by stopping, or at least slowing, the whirlpool we're in. We can start by taking even five minutes at the beginning of the day to try to put things in order. If we don't do this, we'll probably do the first thing that comes up whether it's important or not. Five minutes of deciding what needs to be handled first and what can wait will save us from getting behind on important things. Another five minutes will allow us to decide what we need to handle personally and what we can delegate to someone else. Another ominous sign that we need to watch for in our supervisory job is the tendency to justify doing more and more of the job ourselves, ". . . because I can do it in less time than it takes to explain to or train someone else." When we get into this trap we're doing more and our people are doing less; and they're probably not happy because they see us doing work that they could and should be doing. We're unhappy because we're doing work we shouldn't be doing and we may even decide that our people are lazy or have a poor attitude because they aren't doing more—all because we haven't taken the time to plan our work very well.

Remember, these are indicators we need to be sensitive to; they're not cures. The matter of how we develop is just as important. So far, we've seen that one way is to force ourselves to do five or ten minutes of planning and delegating. Another way is to give ourselves some "instant success." We need confidence in ourselves, and this comes quickest from accomplishing something. Even if the thing we do isn't the biggest or most important job, just finishing a task and stopping long enough to take note of it can boost our confidence. How can we use this technique to our advantage? One simple method is to make a list of the things we have to accomplish in a period of time—a day, a week, or two weeks. If our confidence is fairly low, a day works best. We list the things and number them as they are listed. During the day we mark them off one at a time as we complete them. A good way to mark them off is with a felt-tip pen. This way we can see what job we did and that it has been accomplished. Seeing the broad strokes of the felt pen gives us a boost, because we see that even though the day has been hectic, we've still gotten a few things done. The next day, or at the end of this day, we make a new list, taking the things done off the list and adding new items for the upcoming day. Two things become obvious as we follow this procedure: (1) It shows us how much we are really doing. (2) It gives us practical chances for planning and organizing our work. As we see the things we have to do, we may notice some duplication of effort. We may see that an employee in our unit can do two or three of the items because of the close similiarity between them. Also, as we make our list, we have an incentive to set some priorities. Naturally we want to do the important things first, so they should be near the top of the list. As we list the jobs, we often discover that we've missed some things that should be at the top. If we hadn't made the list in the first place, we'd have missed something important or tried to do it in a hurry at the last minute; in either case we do less than is expected of us. One caution here: it is important to get the right task "size". Writing down something that's going to take two or three days isn't going to build up our sense of achievement; it could have the opposite effect. If we see the list is short and each item takes a day or more, we may need to list some of the parts of the job that can be done separately and then cross these off as we accomplish them. This also serves to organize the large tasks into small, logical steps, helping us do a better job overall while still giving us the sense of frequent "successes."

Another way we can develop is by observing others. First we watch our manager or someone else who is getting a lot of work done in the same amount of time we're working. We study his or her behavior pattern and way of organizing and try to determine what makes that person able to get so much done. We can even discuss the subject with him or her but don't make it a "flattery" session. That person probably gets a lot done by making good use of time, and we don't want to be guilty of taking up too much time with our poor organizational habits. The way to discuss the subject is by asking the right questions, not by asking the person to solve our problems. We watch people work, and then we ask them why they did certain things: "Why did you call the meeting right at that time? What advantage did you gain by having the meeting?" Of course we need to make it clear that we aren't questioning their wisdom, just trying to improve on our own. To improve on our perception we can try to anticipate what their answers will be. We try to figure out the reasoning behind what was done, then see how close we are to the reasons they give. As we get closer and closer, we can see that our judgment is getting better. We're probably making better decisions on our own job now.

Next we make a conscious effort to judge the abilities of our technical and clerical employees. We see how well they accept the responsibilities we give them and make a conscious effort to give them more as they are able to handle them. We aren't trying just to get more work out of them; we're trying to expand their ability to handle more important assignments. Appraising others isn't the easiest thing to do and neither is delegating. However, our ability to do these together is one of the measures of success we can use. There are some who fear giving up responsibility and authority to their employees. Some fear that their subordinates will somehow get the credit and maybe even the job. Such lack of confidence in ourselves can be a sign of poor leadership and immaturity. One common trait of many good leaders is that they attract those who will assume responsibility when it is given. We should bear this in mind when we consider whether or not to let an employee do some of the work or make some of the decisions. Others fear giving up any authority for an even less noble reason; they are afraid that if the job is done wrong, they will have to assume the blame. But remember that a key part of supervision is our willingness to assume the responsibility for our employees in order to give them confidence to take the necessary risks until they have convinced themselves that they really can do well on the job. This doesn't mean that we won't tell the employees when they need to improve, but it does mean that we will be a buffer between them and higher management. It means that we know and will tell them that they did the job well or poorly. Once they develop confidence, they should respond with improved decision-making in their job. If we don't try to create this atmosphere, we're likely to do too much of the work ourselves and ultimately create the very problem we're talking about—not having enough time to do our own job.

THE NEXT JOB?

There are two reasons for developing ourselves: to do better in our present job and to be ready for the next one. It is important to keep them in this order in our mind's eye—the present job, then the next one. This may sound simple enough, but many good supervisors fail to get promoted because they get so interested in the next job that they forget to fulfill the present one properly. We think, talk, and plan about the job we hope to get, while we let the details of the present one slip. Subsequently our interest also begins to wane, and soon a major shortfall occurs in our operation. An important assignment gets only meager attention; details are overlooked and wrong decisions are made; errors creep in and higher management gets involved in finding out what happened. And we, who were potentially able to take on more than we now have assigned, find to our chagrin and embarrassment that we're losing some of the work we used to have because someone up the managerial line doubts our ability to handle even our present job. Some have said, "Do well on the present supervisory assignment, and the future will take care of itself." That's good advice, except that it doesn't include all that's necessary to get ahead. It assumes that the things that are needed on the next managerial job are already in the present one, but this may not be true. If not, then it's well to develop in those areas where we are weak. If the next level above us requires considerable report writing and we don't think we're a good report writer, this is one place we can start. We can look around for books or courses which teach report writing, and we can seek opportunities to do some report writing on our present job. We can start by making short reports on things the manager has asked about, then we work up to longer and more complex ones. Actually doing reports is helpful, but we should also be studying the principles of report writing so our experience will be progressive. We follow the same approach in the other areas where we think the next job exceeds our present skill and knowledge attainments. The advantage of this approach is that it can actually improve our performance on our present assignment. While we are improving in our existing job, and at the same time are improving our supervisory reputation, we are also preparing ourselves to take over a more responsible management assignment when the opportunity arises.

One final word about the next job: Let nature take its course up to a point; don't try to harness and direct it too much. In retrospect, very few people can show where they have been successful at plotting their careers job-for-job. Many successful people will tell us that they got the job by being in the right place at the right time and by being ready when the occasion arose. It's not all luck, but luck admittedly can play a part. Our challenge is to be ready when the luck breaks for us. This means that we not only have developed ourselves to take over the added responsibility, but we have also covered the present one well. Perhaps what this says is that in a real way we help make our luck. Remember that the ways to develop ourselves are too numerous to mention in detail here. We can find out about ways of growing through reading the right books and magazines; there are night schools and self-help courses, there are programs available within many companies and organizations. But these are obvious to most of us; so we won't go into them here—not because they aren't good and profitable, but because they are the obvious things to do when we talk about self-development. We've tried to identify some of the less obvious ones that can complement reading and courses, etc. It might be said that part of the way of telling whether or not we are capable of taking on the next higher assignment is best determined by our ability to perceive the areas and ways of developing ourselves. Successful supervisors, new or old, will be sensitive to their own needs for development and will find ways of making the necessary improvements. More important than that, they will see it as a challenge, not a chore. They will do it and probably call it fun, not drudgery. Good supervision can be learned. If we take the time to step back and look at ourselves and where we are going, we'll see that we have already progressed considerably. It may have been hard work, but that wasn't all it was; there was probably a great deal of fulfillment in making the trip. The rest of the way should be even better!

CONCLUSION

We've already said that appraising employees is a demanding job. An even greater challenge is appraising ourselves. Looking with objective eyes at our own strengths and weaknesses is close to impossible for most of us. One problem is that we know our motives; and when we know that they are good in a certain situation, even though we didn't perform too well, we tend to overlook our weaknesses in that situation. If we're going to improve ourselves, we'll have to be willing to see both the good and the not-so-good in ourselves. We can't be too hard on ourselves, nor too easy. We look at things like time managment, delegation, training, communication, interpersonal skills, etc., and imagine that we are appraising ourselves. We look for a performance standard, then evaluate our actual performance against that standard, not against our intentions. We have another decision to make: Do we want to be better? That sounds like an inane question, but many of us reach a plateau and decide, admitting it or not, that we really don't want to expend the effort or time to raise our performance level any higher. If we make this decision, we should remember it and not end up in the future saying, "I could have had that department manager job if I'd wanted it," or, "I wonder why the organization hasn't treated me better."

On the other hand, if we are serious about being good supervisors—and that certainly is anyone who has read this far—we set some targets for ourselves, decide what must be overcome in order to reach them, and set about getting there. If we look at ourselves and decide that getting to a certain target is too far from our reach at this time, then we set another, short-range target and head for it. Also, if we decide that there are things in the way that aren't under our power to control, then we change our target. Notice that we've used the expression "target" often. We need a target to shoot at, a goal to strive for. It's more than saying, "I'd like to be a better communicator some day." We have to be specific enough to say, "I want to be a better listener within a year." We have to define the weaknesses that are keeping us from getting there, as well as define the goal itself. When we begin to get close to our goal, we'll repeat these questions and decisions to avoid drifting along and not getting any better or any closer to any goal. Remember the proverb we mentioned earlier: "If we don't know where we're going, any road will get us there." That's true of our self-development. The idea is to set a target, then direct our energies toward getting there, remembering that the majority of the successes we have aren't because of somebody else; they're because of us. We don't need "pull" from somebody else in the organization to get ahead as manager. We usually need a little "push" from within ourselves.

EXERCISES

1. Group activity: The entire group should brainstorm a list of things that should be considered in looking at oneself and evaluating present skills. What are the things that need to be looked at? (The list should be recorded, but culled, so that it isn't too long and unwieldy.) Next, how can we determine what our future chances are for upward movement? What are the things we can look at in our own jobs? The group should come up with a manageable list of these, too, and have it recorded for the group to see.

2. Individual activity: Each person should examine the list of notations about his or her present skills. Spend a few minutes using it

and see how specific the points are. Is it really a usable list, or is it too nebulous to be helpful?

3. Group activity: Now that everyone has had a chance to use the list worked up in Exercise 1, see what their reaction is. Brainstorm ways of refining it further until everyone is agreed that it will now give useful data.

4. Individual activity: Each person should now try to use the second list from Exercise 1, the one dealing with things that need to be looked at in our jobs for determining the chances and direction of our future.

5. Group activity: When everyone is finished with Exercise 4, the group should evaluate the list as in Exercise 3. Again the object is to refine the list down to a usable aid in determining where we are going and what it takes to get there. Each person should take both of these lists with them and review them at least annually to measure their progress.

EPILOGUE

We are at the end of another book on how to be a better supervisor. What have we learned? Only time will tell. What has the book tried to offer? We've tried to present a supermarket designed to lay out the possibilities for growth and development. This is not to suggest that everything in the book is applicable to every new supervisor; the suggestions here are just that. There is the possibility that something that has been said will cause the supervisor to get a new idea, a new way of considering an existing problem. When the suggestion and the resulting idea pay off, the time it took to read the book will seem minute.

The authors repeat what has been said earlier: this isn't a rule book; it's a guide book. The ideas and suggestions have all been tried by practical supervisors with enough success to justify their being in this publication. Whether or not they always work for you is not a measure of your effectiveness or your abilities; more likely it's proof that supervising people is complex and commands all of our efforts and skills. If we are willing to put our energies into the job and are willing to learn the skills, then there can be only one result—we'll end up being better supervisors. There may be better ultimate rewards in our career, but this one should suit most of us for a long time to come!

INDEX